Whose Tune Are We Dancing to Anyway?

Published by:
Pavilion Publishing and Media Ltd
Blue Sky Offices
Cecil Pashley Way
Shoreham by Sea
West Sussex
BN43 5FF
Tel: 01273 434 943
Email: info@pavpub.com

Published 2020

A catalogue record for this book is available from the British Library.

ISBN: 978-1-913414-22-1

Pavilion Publishing and Media is a leading publisher of books, training materials and digital content in mental health, social care and allied fields. Pavilion and its imprints offer must-have knowledge and innovative learning solutions underpinned by sound research and professional values.

Authors: Elisabeth Heismann, Deborah Frimpong, Louise Target & Sarah McClay
Production editor: Mike Benge, Pavilion Publishing and Media Ltd.
Cover design: Emma Dawe, Pavilion Publishing and Media Ltd.
Page layout and typesetting: Tony Pitt, Pavilion Publishing and Media Ltd.
Printing: CMP Digital Print Solutions

Contents

Introduction

> *'We came to NVR because we were having difficulties with our daughter. She was involved with a gang in our area and was being exploited sexually. She was always angry, violent towards us, a school refuser and controlled the household. We felt completely helpless; relationships in the family had broken down. We were ashamed of our daughter's behaviour and didn't want others to think badly of her. But the group was lovely; nobody judged us, and everyone was so supportive. We now have more confidence in our parenting skills. Most important of all, we are rebuilding our relationship with our daughter. NVR is not a cure, life with our daughter will always be a challenge, but we are a family once again.'*

This testimony beautifully summarises what we want to bring across in this book. NVR means non-violent resistance, and we understand it in a specific way, the way that it has been elaborated by Haim Omer and others.

NVR is a living practice and the NVR community is constantly evolving, changing and developing new practices. Non-violent resistance is a form of political and social struggle, with the most well-known exponents being Mahatma Gandhi and Martin Luther King, in which people come together to resist oppression through their physical presence and embodied protest (such as occupations, sit-ins, marches and strikes). These concepts have been applied by Haim Omer and others to situations in families and in the community, in which parents or teachers find themselves dealing with children and adolescents who show extreme forms of violent, challenging, non-functional and (self-)destructive behaviour.

The basic idea of this approach is to help the parents, carers or professionals de-escalate conflict and aggressive situations before violence erupts. The focus is not so much on the child's misbehaviour but rather on the helplessness of the adult partners in the communication and on the violent patterns into which they are repeatedly getting drawn.

Some interventions have been elaborated by Haim Omer and his team in Israel such as de-escalation, active resistance, reconciliation gestures, announcements and sit-ins, while new ones have been developed by other practitioners over time in different parts of the world. Many of them are briefly described in the glossary (pages 87 to 92) to help readers who are less familiar with the NVR framework.

In our own work, we (the authors) developed an NVR group approach, as we have found that group members can become instant supporters to each other. After our second group in 2007, we started to invite parents to join new future groups as 'graduate parent facilitators'. In 2017, we started training some of the more seasoned parents who had worked with us over many years as parent mentors, so they could support new parent facilitators when making the transition from graduate parent. We have found the combination of group work and mentoring, along with the inclusion of parent facilitators with lived experience to be highly effective and have presented our results in numerous national and international contexts.

This book aims to give readers, many of whom may be unfamiliar with NVR in general, or with this way of working in particular, an idea of why we feel it works so well for parents. While most books on NVR practice have been written by professionals, where parents' voices may perhaps feature in the context of a case vignette or brief testimony, newcomers to the approach might welcome this book which has been co-written by parents who have been involved in NVR group projects for many years, so they can learn how NVR works straight from the horse's mouth[1].

The four co-authors of this book are three parents with lived experience of using NVR and a family therapist who has used the approach for 14 years working with parents in Child and Adult Mental Health services for over 25 years and who now works freelance providing training. The purpose of this collaborative book is to highlight and demonstrate the experience and impact of parent participation in NVR.

Living and delivering NVR in one of London's most polarised boroughs[2] in terms of the distribution of wealth and deprivation, where gang problems, knife crime and child sexual exploitation (CSE) are rife, the challenges faced by the three parent authors are representative of some of the issues many families experience throughout London and the UK[3]. All four co-authors have worked extensively with parents, families, young people and communities, who often do not voluntarily access or collaborate with

1 Other publications by parents exist outside the NVR context. One which we feel a particular affinity with is *The Cry of the Brave and Broken-hearted Parent* (Pace, 2019) from the organisation PACE (Parents Against Child Exploitation) about the impact of CSE.

2 The South London borough where we live and worked was the 19th most deprived out of 326 local authorities in the UK in 2010 (Hines, 2012). Of the working age residents in the borough, 4.8% were claiming job seekers allowance, of which 12% were of the age group below 24 and of which 37% had been claiming for more than six months (Hines, 2012). The borough was ranked fourth highest out of 32 London boroughs for assault and third highest for injury offences. The report 'Strategy for Tackling Serious Youth Violence Report' (unpublished), which was created by the borough's Safer Community department as a strategy paper for discussion in the borough's Serious Youth Violence Panel, stated that youth crime accounted for 49.2% of crimes.

3 The study of Ollefs, Schlippe, Omer and Kriz (2009) showed that most of the parents were suffering from severe depression, which would have required clinical treatment, before taking part in the program. The indicators for depression went down to average after treatment. Our findings in three boroughs of the 400 families who attended our generic 15 groups between 2006 and 2015 support these results.

existing services such as social care, child mental health services and education, not wanting to 'dance to their tune'. Having experienced so many injustices in their lives, individuals and families feel judged, blamed and pathologised and have a deep-seated mistrust of all people in authority who have too often let them down. They have developed an 'us versus them' attitude that applies to all forms of authority.

We also come across the opposite: people who have a blind faith in any expert or person in power. In our experience, young people pick up their parents' feelings and attitudes, often deepening the experience of feeling disenfranchised. Our work – as we hope to demonstrate in this book – has made a significant impact in improving relationships for many of these young people and their families, first and foremost within the family itself, as well as with the outside world.

After completing NVR groups, many parents and young people report that their relationships with professionals improved significantly and they feel less marginalised in their contact with them. One parent felt so empowered that she retook control of her own life and her own affairs and wrote an announcement to her family doctor about her concerns in relation to her child, with the immediate positive effect of getting her child assessed in due course. Therefore – apart from the over 400 families that have benefited from NVR groups in our area and about who the lead co-ordinators have collected and audited demographic and outcome data – local services, even those that are not directly involved in delivering NVR programs, are now also passionately advocating the approach. This helps to increase the visibility of NVR in our boroughs and beyond. Almost a third of London boroughs have started investing in this approach and adapted it to their specific needs and some inter-borough-networking around NVR has begun to take place.

The four authors are convinced that a collective NVR approach can best develop a more compassionate, collaborative, egalitarian and aware community, which can then respond, and not purely react, to the needs of young people with severe emotional, behavioural and mental health difficulties and their families. For us, this means actively involving parents in the design and delivery of NVR programmes. In our way of developing the NVR-approach, we were influenced by Paulo Freire's (1972)[4] basic idea of a critically conscious community that can only be created and sustained when

4 See Freire (1972): We are particularly interested in Freire's concept of participatory education that he developed in 1970 for adult literacy programs in Brazil. The aim of his method of conscientisation was to help adult learners of literacy to 'read the world' alongside 'reading the words'. The literacy programmes are designed to help learners develop critical consciousness through critical thinking styles to overcome obstacles and problems and transform their reality through critical reflection, dialogue and co-operation with teachers and each other, giving them agency in their own lives.

parents with 'lived experience', practitioners and organisations, all work together and feel equally responsible and passionate about their duty of care towards young people and the communities in which they live. Reflection is acted on as they perceive their situation no longer as 'limiting', but as 'challenging', thereby 'externalising' their problems.

This very much fits with Helmut Rosa's (Rosa, 2019) concept of self-efficiency in resonance, which will be described in more detail in Part 4 of this book, and with Michael White's and David Epston's narrative approach (White, 1989; White & Epston, 1990), and with their approach of externalising difficult stories and exploring alternative empowering narratives, thereby 're-authoring problem-saturated stories' into those of empowerment and personal agency, which will give people the tools to 'intervene in their world'.

A further development of narrative practice is the concept of Insider Witnessing Practice (Epston, 2016), which allows people to experience and observe themselves by witnessing a performance of a particular aspect of their story, becoming both an 'insider' and an 'outsider' to their own story and allowing them to watch the performative enactment of their own experience as 'me but not me' (Carlson & Epston, 2017). All the above influences have informed and complemented the way we practice NVR.

A word of thanks

We are immensely grateful to a wide network of parents, professionals and organisations, who have all equally contributed to the growth and successes of NVR and with whom we have collaborated and who have inspired us enormously with their feedback and suggestions over the years.

Of course, we learned the NVR key concepts from many people, who are mentioned throughout this book by name and from all the others that we may not have named. We cannot cite all the literature that describes the NVR concepts and applications that have been developed over the years in many different countries.

To the German-speaking reader, we explicitly recommend the books of Omer & von Schlippe, 2004; 2010; Grabbe *et al*, 2013, Weinblatt, 2013; Ollefs, 2017, and the comprehensive recent handbook of Körner *et al*, 2019.

In our embodied and performance-based work with parents and professionals, we are deeply indebted to the work of Augusto Boal and his theatre of the oppressed, to Jakob Moreno's psychodrama and therapeutic action model, and to the many embodied exercises that we picked up in workshops and conferences, such as mirroring from Uri Weinblatt,

(Weinblatt, 2007; 2014; 2019) and embodying parental and professional presence from Bruno Koerner and Martin Lemme (Lemme & Koerner, 2018; Lemme *et al*, 2019).

Part 1: Why we write about parent participation in this book

We are deeply committed to the continuous development of NVR practices, making them more accessible, transparent, participatory and adaptable to the lives and relationships of those in our communities, who are suffering from the de-humanising effects of deprivation and poverty, isolation, injustice, oppression and racism. We therefore wrote this book to give some lived examples of how and why parent participation in NVR has worked for us and for others we came in contact with, hoping to inspire readers to follow our participatory approach.

Elisabeth will start the testimonies, briefly describing how she came across the theories and concepts of participation in her lived experience and subsequently experimented with applying them to NVR parenting work, particularly in NVR parent groups and the training of professional facilitators. Each of the three parents will then describe how they and their families found their way out of extremely challenging situations and, using NVR interventions, managed to overcome their problems and developed self-efficiency.

Each of their stories highlights those NVR ideas and skills that were significant in helping them and their family to change their situation. However, their stories of improvement did not stop when their own lives had become liberated from the grip of helplessness and hopelessness. All three decided to commit themselves to the wider NVR community, making their testimonies available to new parents and to professionals, thus participating in co-creating and embodying the effectiveness of the NVR approach.

Our shared and lived NVR practices have consistently confirmed and extended the existing NVR model. In part 3 we reflect and discuss commonalities and differences between the experiences of the three parents and why we think NVR worked for them and others. In Part 4 we will discuss how and why we feel parent participation works, and in Part 5 we describe in more detail the different areas in which graduate parents are, or have been, involved.

This is followed by the glossary of NVR terms (pages 87 to 92), which was developed by Elisabeth Heismann, Julia Jude and Liz Day (Heismann *et al*, 2019). The final pages of the book contain suggestions for further reading and books that explain the wider context, which would have disturbed the flow of the text. You can also find a list of references and websites that we refer to in the text at the back.

The appendix contains two chapters about parent participation and one chapter about the specialist NVR group work also taken from *Non-Violent Resistance: Innovations in practice* (Heismann *et al*, 2019).

Part 2: The authors' stories about their participation in NVR

Elisabeth's story about co-creating participation in NVR

I was born in Germany only five years after the Second World War, thereby belonging to the generation of 1968 that rebelled against any form of repression, social injustice and re-armament, and supported worldwide movements against oppression, colonialism, apartheid and social injustices. In the 1970s I became aware of Latin American liberation theology[5] and the community and education practices that were based on the understanding that peace cannot be attained without the complete liberation and de-colonising of the people.

Many Latin-American priests, politicians, educators, poets and musicians and the communities that they had influenced, were convinced of the need for revolutionary changes in their countries and refused to be intimidated by the power of dictators or traditional hierarchies, but followed their conscience and faith instead, often with terrible consequences, including death, exile and imprisonment, such as befell Salvador Allende, Pablo Neruda, Francisco Javier Varela García in Chile, Paulo Freire and Augusto Boal in Brazil, and Ignazio Martín-Baró and Óscar Romero in El Salvador.

Ernesto Cardenal was a charismatic liberation priest and poet who lived and worked in a very small community in Solentiname in Nicaragua in the late 1970s. As their local priest, he held dialogues with the literate and illiterate indigenous people in his church every Sunday about the gospels, and how they reflected their world of being poor and oppressed peasants under the dictatorship of Somoza. He shared with them the ideas of Latin American revolutionary theology, that God sides with the poor and the oppressed and does not like injustice and inequality. This prepared them to redress injustice in social action. When in 1977 Cardenal occupied a military barracks together with local farmers on the small island of

5 Latin American Liberation Theology was the political praxis of Latin American theologians and priests such as Gustavo Gutiérrez of Peru, Leonardo Boff of Brazil, Ernesto Cardenal in Nicaragua, Óscar Romera and Ignacio Martín-Baró in San Salvador in the 1970s, who all applied the gospel to the political situation of oppression and poverty in Latin America, often with the result of personal persecution and murder like in the cases of Romera and Martín-Baró.

Solentiname to protest against the Nicaraguan dictator Somoza, it resulted in the complete destruction of their church and village.

I was emotionally very moved when I visited this small community in Nicaragua and Salvador Allende's grave in Santiago in Chile a couple of years ago.

Later, when trained as a family therapist, I came across the writings and practices of the narrative therapists Michael White and David Epston, who had dedicated their work to liberating individuals and groups from oppressive, pathologising and highly determining stories and enabling them to 're-author' their lives and thereby take control of them again. Michael White explains how dominant (negative) and problem-saturated stories have led people to 'stuckness', blaming and failure. Externalising them makes space for 'alternative stories' that are developed in co-operation with others and allow the authors of these negative stories to take action and 'retrieve their lives', reclaiming them from the grip of previously dominant stories. This personal agency gives people the tools to 'intervene in their world' (White & Epston, 1990, pp61-65).

The 'Just Therapy' team in New Zealand approached the narrative ideas from a cultural and socio-economic angle, challenging gender, culture, socio-economic justice and differential power in New Zealand and the Pacific Islands. The New Zealand, Pacific Island and Samoan partners of the Just Therapy Group work closely with their local minority communities in all their therapeutic work, in research and in their work with the New Zealand government. They look at the key local cultural and historical values that sustain communities and weave them together, focusing on their ethics, liberative narratives and practices, and on their ways of non-hierarchical relating to build partnerships and redress colonialism and injustice. When I visited them in New Zealand with a friend, we witnessed and experienced this approach, when the multi-cultural team fed back research results to the commissioning government officials. The research investigated volunteering in the Pacific Islands during the Second World War and the feedback presentation started with saying prayers and singing songs in several different indigenous Pacific Island languages. These performances fitted with the questions: whose ideas were informing the research? In whose interest, and for whose benefit did it take place? Who controlled the process and decided on the results?

In summary, I learned from all the above people and their writings and practices that social and personal liberation, decolonisation, conscientisation (Freire, 1972), transformation and change cannot be prescribed or dictated, but can only happen when based on the lived experience and co-creation of those who they should benefit. This noncontrolling, non-external expert approach aims for inter-connectedness, mutuality and participation, working *with* and not *for* people, which requires acceptance, respect, trust, perseverance, compassion, love and forgiveness of all parties involved.

Forty Professionals from our trust attended a training day with Haim Omer in Canterbury in 2005 and a fewer of us had a two-day workshop with Uri Weinblatt in Margate in 2006. After the training with Haim Omer, I immediately saw the potential of the NVR ideas and their applicability to the families that we worked with, particularly in combination with the liberation and narrative approaches described earlier.

We created a steering group and wrote our first parent booklet (Day *et al*, 2007), which we had designed to explain to parents Haim Omer's manual on NVR (Omer, 2004) using simple language and with many illustrations. In March 2006, our first pilot parent group was launched, together with the publication of this first parent booklet. After our second parent group, the idea of including 'graduate parents' became natural and possible. Parents who had attended more than five weeks of a total of 12 were called 'graduate parents' and were asked to participate in new groups as parent facilitators. Parent participation subsequently became the most unique feature of our NVR parent groups, equally liked by professionals, new parents and 'graduate parents'. For me, parent participation has been a most transformative experience. Parents became human beings and friends rather than remaining within the clinical boundaries of 'clients'.

I have learned so much from them and I value their love, humour generosity and common sense. The experience of working with them, having an insight into their family lives over several years, and our passionate interactions in multiple contexts has changed me into more humble and compassionate person in the sense of Erich Fromm's art of loving[6], enabling me to step into their shoes and see things from their perspective.

Sarah's story and participation in NVR

There is light at the end of the tunnel. From an early age, my son had shown challenging behaviour. As a single-parent family, we were always involved with Child and Adolescent Mental Health Services (CAMHS) in relation to my son's behaviour between the ages of five and 17, attending many family therapy sessions. Unfortunately, these sessions were not successful – my son would sit in the room, hear how his behaviour upset

6 Eric Fromm sees love as a 'commitment' without 'guarantee', as an 'act of faith', which can also exist beyond one's family and be committed towards those with whom one is in contact with through one's work. He believes that loving is incompatible with the principles underlying capitalist societies with their constantly changing structures, but based on the humanness of our nature, as it requires stability and commitment (Fromm, 1959).

me, listen and become aware of my weaknesses and then, once we were home, he would use this to his advantage.

As the years passed and my son became an adolescent, he would no longer attend family therapy sessions. As a parent, I was not coping at all. From the age of 15 my son would be extremely violent towards me and his younger sister. The more I tried to discipline him, the worse he became. Each day was like walking on eggshells around the house. Our house was no longer a loving family home – it was a war zone. Our home was ruled by his violence. My daughter and I were frightened of my son.

When I did not give in to my son's demands, he would swear and tower over me, shouting abuse into my face, pinning me against the wall and holding my arms so tightly that I would bruise. He would lock me in the bathroom by holding the door handle on the other side, so I would be pulled off the seat.

My daughter has learning difficulties which caused a speech delay. Each time she tried to speak, her brother would say: 'Mm, come on, hurry up, get your words out, ya retard'. My daughter also was punched by her brother, shut in between the door and hit, and had pillows held over her face with force, so, at times, she could not breathe. Every time my daughter walked past her brother, she would flinch.

As a parent, I felt helpless. I could not protect myself or my daughter from my son's violence. I spent my days in fear of him. So I spent my days crying and feeling isolated, because no one could help me. This was our life, day in and day out.

Then, one day, when he was 16, I picked up the phone and called 999. The police came and arrested my son for criminal damages to our house. As a parent, this took a lot for me to do. In the past, I had always threatened to call the police but never seen it through. It was horrible to see my son in handcuffs and put into a police car, but at the same time it was a relief, and I knew I had acted in the best way possible.

Myself and my daughter were put on the at-risk register, and then social services became involved to offer support. I did not allow my son back home. He stayed with my parents until I decided I wanted him back.

The social worker called one day and mentioned the NVR parent group. I remember being so rude to her saying: 'No, I am not interested in doing another parent group. It is not me who has the problem. It is my son'. Over the years, I had grown to hate him. Because of his violence all the love I had once felt for him had slowly been chipped away.

Anyway, the good news is that I did the NVR group in the end… At that time my son had turned 17.

I did not think this NVR parent group was going to be of any help at all, as in the past I had attended parent groups and they had gone nowhere. But I went along with an open mind and showed a willingness to learn the NVR principles, and then went home and put the NVR tools into practice. This was very different to other parent groups that I had attended and was working for me because it had role plays, which were extremely helpful as they gave me a good insight how to use NVR. I could get a real feel for a situation when doing a role play, so that I was confident to put things into practice when a challenging situation at home arose.

In the beginning it was difficult to understand the principles of NVR, because it felt as if I was ignoring the bad behaviours and not disciplining my son the way that I normally would have done.

This felt alien to me, as I always acted on the bad behaviour, as and when it happened. NVR taught me that this would cause escalation between myself and my son. It is far better to act on the bad behaviour at a later time, following the principle of de-escalation: 'Strike when the iron is cold' (see glossary, p87).

I remember saying to myself: 'I am not ignoring the bad behaviour. I am choosing to act on it later, when things are calmer'. At first this was very difficult to do, and I did have times when I slipped back to my old ways. The important thing was that I noticed this and remembered to de-escalate the next time.

When learning about the baskets (see glossary, p87), I felt I could breathe again. A weight had been lifted, as I only had to focus on the small basket behaviour. I could compromise or leave the medium basket for now and wait to act on it once I had resolved the small basket behaviour. I learned that the large basket contained all the things that annoyed me but were not important to worry about and which I could ignore. By not reacting to the large basket behaviours (i.e. swearing, untidy bedroom etc.), I noticed over a couple of weeks that they began to stop re-occurring, as I did not seem to be nagging at my son constantly over every little thing, as I had usually done.

When I had written my announcement (see glossary, p87) I still did not feel love for my son. The relationship had so far gone, I remember, that I did not want to make it sound loving and affectionate. I wanted it to sound strong and to show him that I was taking back my control as his mum and that I really meant what I wrote. I kept it short and to the point, as if it was too wordy he would have lost interest in reading it. I remember the words: 'I will no longer tolerate…'. I thought this sounded so powerful and assertive as it used words that I would have never thought of normally using.

'I will no longer tolerate your violent behaviour!'

The day I gave my announcement, it really empowered me as a parent. I was now making my stand as a parent. This is how I reclaimed my parental presence (glossary, p87). I still did not feel comfortable to read my announcement out loud in front of him, as I know that my voice would have let me down by sounding nervous and shaky. So I left it on his bed for him to read. I did not mention it to my son on the next day, as the NVR principles are to deliver your announcement, waiting to see what the response is and not getting into an argument, as all this causes escalation. I could tell that he had read it, because the next day his behaviour was different, a lot calmer.

My first announcement to my 17-year-old son:

> *Dear...*
>
> *As from today, I am going to make changes. I will no longer tolerate your violent behaviour towards your sister and myself. I will no longer keep your violence a secret from family and friends. I am not trying to control you. I want to re-build our relationship and have a happy, loving home. I am your mum. I love you, and I want the best for you.*
>
> *Love Mum*

My supporters (glossary, p87) were the other parents of the NVR group. As attending the group was my time to speak freely, I did not let my son know that I was attending it. It was something for me.

I know that if I had told my son that I was doing NVR, he would have used this to his advantage, just like in the past with family therapy. Each time I would try to de-escalate the situation, he would continue escalating it. I had a long-term non-residential partner, but I wanted to keep our relationship problem-free. I felt that I should put all the effort into my family, giving up most of my time for my children. I had my mum as my supporter. Every time I needed her she would be at the other end of the phone, reminding me to be persistent: 'Go for a walk until he calms down!' She would let me know when I was slipping a bit and escalating the situation again.

She looked after my daughter so that I could attend each week. If my son had been less violent in one week, my mum would call him to say that she was pleased to hear that he had been nicer to his sister and say how pleased she was that he was really trying to be less violent.

My son continued to go through my bag and steal money from my purse. I would use active resistance (glossary, p87) and walk around the house, carrying my bag on my shoulder while I washed up or answered the front door. I even took my handbag to the bathroom and slept with it in my bed, wrapped around my arm at night. By doing this I was making my son aware that I knew he was taking my money from my bag, but I was not accusing him directly. My actions were speaking louder than words. In the past I would have shouted and accused him of being a thief, which would have caused escalation and, as a result, he would have punched holes in the walls from being ashamed[7].

In 2014 I attended a conference in Greenwich with Uri Weinblatt on shame, and I became aware that blaming another person can lead to shame. I remember Uri saying that even though shame is an emotion that can be

7 In the context of NVR, Uri Weinblatt has written extensively about how too much or too little shame can be experienced between parents and children and how the regulation of shame enables connection and reconnection (Weinblatt, 2013; 2016; 2018; 2019).

good, as it helps us to make good choices, it can also become an unhealthy emotion when it leads to making another person feel that they are to blame.

Uri said that if someone feels they are to blame, they will feel shame and may stay away from others in order to avoid being further blamed or become angry as a result of being held responsible and shamed. This rang alarm bells for me; I could really relate to what Uri was saying as it had happened between myself and my son. He would do something, I would be quick to blame him for his unacceptable behaviour, which would bring about shame in my son. I now realise how unhealthy this pattern between us has been, as a child/young person cannot cope with the emotion of 'shame'.

Because I did not want to place blame upon him for his actions and shame him, I did not put the sit-In tool into practice with my son – I found it too confrontational.

In my opinion the 'connecting conversations' (see glossary, p87) resulting from the 'connection before correction' principle, are more effective than the sit-in (glossary, p87). They are two-way conversations that resolve situations without escalation or putting blame or shame on the child/young person.

My main tools which changed our relationships were all those which connected us.

For example, as a result of the reconciliation gestures, my relationship with him switched from a hateful one to a loving one. I demonstrated to him that – even when he was showing unacceptable behaviour – I still loved him. My love is unconditional. In the beginning, this was extremely difficult for me to do, because I would be fuming with him, when he kicked holes in the walls. The last thing I wanted to do, was to put a reconciliation gesture in place for him. After a while this did get easier to do and I began to get delight from giving them, as my son would be thinking: 'What is wrong with mum? I have just kicked her wall and she has tidied my bedroom and text me, "I love you"?'

In the past I would have held a grudge and not spoken to him for a week.

By the end of the NVR parent group our family was transformed. We were much happier. Our house had become a calm environment. I had regained my parental presence in our house and had regained a loving relationship with my son. Life was much happier. I felt confident in my ability to be the parent my children needed. I was pleased I did the parent group. NVR gave me back my parental presence in the home back, reduced the violence from recurring and rebuilt my relationship with my son.

Two-years after doing the NVR parent group

One evening the police knocked at the door with a warrant to search the house. My son had been picked up by the police and arrested for possession of class A drugs with intent to supply. I was shocked. How could this be? There were no signs. This was my worst nightmare. I thought we had overcome the worst, but how wrong I was. This situation was much harder than his previous violence within our home. This situation, I felt, was completely out of my control. How was I ever going to get through this?

His criminal behaviour had been going on for a while and I had obviously been a 'naïve parent', unaware of him hanging out with the wrong crowd in the street. I carried guilt for a while, as I knew that I was partly to blame. I had lost my parental presence and the relationship with him again. I remembered that another important principle of NVR is not to hold on to blame and guilt, as it gets in the way of moving forward. As a parent, I am more that familiar with this process. This is how I had lost my parental presence in the first place and then over-compensated to make up for all the guilt I was holding onto. I now tell myself when guilt sneaks up: 'I cannot change the past, but I can make changes for the future'. This helps me to shift guilt, shame and blame.

Due to doing the NVR two years earlier, I had no doubt in my mind that NVR would not fail me this time around either. I used all my NVR knowledge to win my son back from the gang he was involved with. I had just re-built my relationship with him and was not going to give up on him now that we had come so far. NVR had empowered me enough that I felt like I could take on the world outside. I was no longer the parent who would sit back and not act on a challenging situation.

Whenever I went in my son's bedroom and found any drugs, I would remove them and hold on to them. I could not throw them away as this would have put him in great danger from other gang members. When he went to his room, he would notice them missing and would have to ask me about their whereabouts. This made him aware that I knew what he was up to. I made sure that I did not escalate the situation. When he asked for them, I would give them back to him and say in a firm calm way: 'I do not want you to bring them back into the house again!'

When my son was out and did not answer his phone, I would ring the people he was hanging out with in the streets – I had found their numbers in my son's bedroom. This was demonstrating my parental presence in the street. My son would soon start to answer his phone when I rang him because the last thing a gang wants is to be pestered by a parent. They like to keep a low profile.

I also used reconciliation gestures to win my son back from the gang: inviting him to my mum's house for dinner on a Sunday, which is our family day. This took a lot of persistence as my son would always refuse, but eventually one day he agreed. I would also ask him to do jobs in the garden for me and at my mum's house. Making him feel important, I would say: 'You do that so good. I could have never dug that hole without your help'. I would mention to my friends how much help he was in front of him so that he could hear me sing his praises and feel important that he had a purpose in our family home and that I valued him as my son. Sometimes it felt I had got him back for a while, only to find out later I hadn't. This was the worst feeling. I felt so disheartened, because I had worked so hard to try and change things for the better. NVR taught me to keep a positive mind: 'Persist, Resist, Unite and Repair'.

As we now had now developed a better relationship, I was encouraged to do a sit-in (glossary, p87) with my son, whereas in the past, when he was violent in the home, I had not dared doing one.

This sit-in was based on the concept 'Connection before Correction'. By doing it I was not blaming my son or judging him. I chose my wording carefully. In the past, I would have blamed and judged him. But I knew that if I blamed or judged him, the situation would escalate and we would not resolve anything or move on from it in a calm non-confrontational way.

Using active resistance (glossary, p87), I took the door key from my son so that he had to come home at 11pm, after which the door would be locked and he would have to arrange to stay at a friend's house. I made another announcement when he was 19.

My second announcement:

> *'On Sunday, 24th February, you brought six little bags of cocaine into our house, despite my wishes in an earlier conversation regarding drugs in the house. I cannot accept this, and I told you on two occasions before that I will take further action and you will need to leave, should this happen again. I have decided to give you 28 days to abide by the following rules:*
>
> *No drugs of any kind to be brought into the house.*
>
> *The front door to be locked by 11pm, and if you are any later than 11pm you will have to arrange to sleep somewhere else.*
>
> *You no longer have the front door key.*

> *You will sign on with job seekers allowance.*
>
> *I am not doing this to control you. I am doing this, because I love you and I do not want to see you in prison or dead.*
>
> *If you cannot abide by these rules, you will need to move out. I will support you with this as much as I can to help you, i.e. get you a contact number for the housing department, which will accommodate you within 24 hours.'*

I remember being full of tears and with a lump in my throat, as I wrote this announcement, thinking: 'how did my son ever get to this point?' No parent ever wants to throw their son out. I think that is what gave me the strength to keep fighting and never give up on him. I wanted to show him that I was there as his mum, in good times and bad, no matter what. Giving up would have been the easier way out for me. By using the NVR principles of standing my ground and keeping a positive attitude, I got through this difficult nightmare.

NVR is brilliant: its principles can be adapted to specific situations in all aspects of family life, inside and outside the home. It is not a magic wand. Parents must stay persistent and follow the NVR principles in order to see the positive effects it brings about.

When facilitating in NVR parent groups, new parents are inspired when hearing how I used the NVR tools to improve life at home. I explain how I used active resistance by walking around the house, washing up, having a bath and going to bed with my handbag attached to me. Other parents can relate to this and are very keen to use my experiences within their own household. I explain to the parents that my actions speak louder than words. I did not accuse my son. However, he could see that I always carried my handbag with me in the house, and he fully understood why. This was effective as I was doing something about the unacceptable behaviour without escalating the situation.

I explain to parents that active resistance (glossary, p87) had changed my old parenting pattern. Another example of how I used this NVR principle was when my son came home drunk one night. He was sick all over the living room floor and left it for me to clear up. I was really annoyed with him. This was very disrespectful. I chose to bite my tongue and decided to hide his door key, knowing full well that he would not remember where he had left it that night when he was in no fit state. I went to bed with a smile as I felt I had taught him a lesson. The next morning, he asked where his key was. I replied by saying, 'I don't know; where did you leave it?' After an hour of him looking for it, I said: 'I've found your key under your trainers'.

Parents really enjoy hearing this story, but at times ask whether this would have escalated the situation. I explain it would only have escalated matters if my son had been aware that I had deliberately not revealed the location of his keys. I see this course of action as coming from a parent who wants to show her son that there will be natural consequences for his actions. And from that night onwards he never came home in a drunken state again.

Parents at times feel that their children take them for granted and are at a loss as to how to improve this. They are inspired by this example and come up with their own ideas to change their old parenting pattern. This may be leaving the washing laying around the floor so that the young person learns that, if they do not pick up their dirty washing and put it in the laundry basket, it will not get washed.

I often read a mindfulness visualisation (glossary, p87) that helps parents to relax and take care of themselves at the end of an NVR parenting group, and to develop a non-judgemental and non-violent stance towards themselves and others before they go back home and face up to new challenges. Once a parent came to me and said, 'This was so relaxing, would you mind if I take that mindfulness exercise home to use with my son?' He had autism and ADHD and she thought that it would help him to settle at bedtime.

Before new parents start an NVR Parent group, I sometimes meet with them and tell them my story of how things were and how we are now as a family. They are very keen to listen and ask many questions, which I always answer honestly. By seeing me in person, no longer a broken parent but full of confidence, this is very inspiring for them. This encourages them to go ahead and do the NVR parent group. On several occasions, parents came up to me and said: 'You really inspired us to do the parent group. Thank you. We would not have done it if it weren't for you telling us your story.'

When mentoring an NVR Graduate parent who had started as a new parent facilitator, I could see from the improvement in her personal well-being, self-esteem and confidence, that I had been an inspiration for her. In the beginning she had shown a lot of self-doubt in her abilities, but over the weeks I saw a dramatic change in her. Experiences like these make my role as an NVR volunteer worthwhile. It is very rewarding to be part of these processes of positive change.

When I attend NVR training days and conferences, I also share my stories of how life once was and how NVR has helped me to grow into a positive parent. I often mention how I used NVR to win my son back from gang involvement and criminal activity, and how reconciliation gestures helped rebuild our relationship and led to unconditional love for each other, no matter how bad things had got in the past. Again and again, professionals tell me afterwards that I inspired them to the point that they also want to put NVR into their personal practice with the parents they support.

When I was involved in an adult mental health ward, I shared my knowledge of NVR with the staff members, particularly the self-announcement (glossary, p87) and how it can shift guilt and blame, which so many parents hold onto. They were very interested in the self-announcement and how it can be worded in a way that helps most patients with PTSD to get rid of any negative thoughts that they all have. Once they understood how all the NVR tools can be used for a positive outlook for the future, the staff were amazed and soon realised that this could also become a way forward in adult mental health on their wards.

When my children showed signs of unhealthy sibling rivalry, I used reconciliation gestures (glossary, p87) to rebuild their relationship. When explaining this to parents and professionals, they are all very inspired and want to give it a try. I explain that, at times, it is important to think outside the box within the NVR framework. In my view, the good thing about NVR is that it is very adaptable to each individual situation and for different people.

I explain to others that my children were not aware when I applied the reconciliation gestures. I would, for example, say to my daughter, 'Offer your brother some chocolate; he'd like that', even if they had been arguing that day. When my daughter needed something fixed, I would ask her brother to do it for her. This showed my daughter that her brother has a nice, kind side to him. I also encouraged my children to have a movie night together, sitting in the same room. I had to be persistent with this and things did not improve overnight between them. However, their bickering and fighting has now completely stopped, and I can leave the room without worrying about them, have a bath in peace and even stay out the odd night.

Where are we today? We are still on track with a calm home life. My son is now 27 and has not had any involvement with the gang for over three years. For walking away from the gang he suffered a beating, and I, as his mum, had to pick up the pieces. This is what young people do not understand: gang involvement has a ripple effect, and you never fully get your life back, as you will always have to look over your shoulder. He now works doing construction, which he really enjoys. I am so proud of how far he has come and how he has turned his life around. This was not easy for him or for me.

Deborah's story and participation in NVR

Ever since I could remember, I liked working with children, and when I was 18 years old I knew that I wanted to get married and have my own. I did not imagine that the God I believed in would eventually bless me with nine children. I was born in the UK but lived in Canada for 25 years, before returning for 22 years. My oldest at the time of writing this report is 31 years old, while my youngest turned 10 in May. I have four boys and four girls, and a stepdaughter. I never envisioned the unpredictable journey that lay ahead. Looking back, the unexpected early arrival of my second daughter may have been an indication of what the days ahead would be like. I was eager to raise my children in a happy home, even though I had had a very authoritarian upbringing. My mother did her best as a married woman who ended up raising her three children as a single mum. This article primarily highlights my challenges and ongoing journey with my second daughter.

Before I was introduced to NVR, I raised the children with the help of my husband in a very authoritarian manner ('our way or you are in trouble') – this was the way we had both been brought up. My husband came from an African background, which I later found out affected and limited his understanding of the English word 'empathy', the ability to understand and share the feelings of another. I came from a mixed African and Caribbean upbringing which, in addition to biblical influences as I got older, caused me to believe that children should not speak back or be disrespectful to their parents and those in authority. I believed in what the Bible says: 'children obey your parents the way the Lord wants, this is the right thing to do' and the command that says: 'Honour your father and mother'. We corrected our children at times using harsh punishments, which for the most part *did* seem to help them stay on track, or so we believed.

However, our second daughter became more defiant and rebellious. I thought at one point, 'How far do the punishments have to go to get her to behave "properly"?' By the age of 10 she had got into trouble at school and was having a lot of peer relationship issues, which she was not sharing with us. On the outside, she appeared very confident, but in hindsight I now realise it was a cover for the pain and hurt of being bullied and ridiculed for being slightly overweight.

She started running away from home, and this became more frequent until social services got involved. After several years of a repeated pattern of running away (at least 32 times), in August 2014 the social worker suggested taking the specialist NVR course. However, by that time I had completely lost trust in the social worker, because she had made a grave mistake by advising our daughter that, whenever she was frustrated and didn't want to come home, she should send a message to her older sister via social media, which on one occasion she did. It resulted in our daughter going missing for a week with some irreversible life changing consequences. At this point I was devastated by the draining feelings of hopelessness, of not knowing when and where my daughter was, which meant putting herself at risk of being sexually exploited. I believed *she* needed help, not *me*.

At this point the family was feeling the constant scrutiny of social services, which was very invasive. As a result of mistrusting the social worker and the police, who seemed unhelpful, I decided to attend the NVR course after a few months because I thought that attending the course would help us get social services 'off our back'. We were desperate for change.

There had been many opportunities for us to put blame on the government, which we felt had let us down by taking the authority of parenting 'out of our hands' by allowing younger children to get condoms even though the age of sexual consent is 16. I believe that these mixed messages to young people result in their lacking respect for their parents.

At this very low point in my life, I also experienced heart failure and was diagnosed with a life-threatening heart condition. I felt my faith in God was really being put to the test.

In October 2014, I began the NVR journey with very few expectations but perhaps an ounce of hope, which the bible describes as 'faith as little as a mustard seed, but God is able to work with it'. After one home visit and two visits at a café, I started the NVR journey. My husband and I had to do a lot of shuffling to manage for me to attend the 14-week course because four of the other children attended swimming lessons on the same evening as the NVR course, but we felt, at this point, we had nothing to lose.

When I walked in on the first day, I was grateful to see a familiar face: one of the graduate parents that had come to one of the café visits. She smiled and made me feel welcome. Initially I thought I would just attend one class and leave. However, the written messages from previous graduate parents, which we read out loud, helped me to go back each week. The message read: 'Stay with it, it works'. I honestly did not think the course was going to help me, but if it somehow could help my daughter, it would be worth it.

Week after week I turned up to the course, each time learning another NVR tool to use. In the first half of each of our sessions, we usually had a specialist speaker from agencies that work with young people who had put themselves at risk, who gave us useful information. Afterwards we were introduced to the NVR concepts of de-escalation (not allowing triggers to upset us – see glossary, p87), parental presence (being present in our children's decisions, even when we were not with them – see glossary p87) and baskets (having the privilege to only focus on two of the most challenging behaviours according to Grabbe's four parenting values – see glossary, p87 – in the first few sessions). I found that these tools on their own were great initial skills in fighting back hopelessness. They allowed me to 'strike while the iron is cold' (see glossary, de-escalation, p87) and sift through the many issues, prioritising them and narrowing them down to two unacceptable behaviours that connected to the four parental values (glossary, p87), which we were reintroduced to. It was powerful. The other issues would still be addressed, but at a later time. I could already breathe a sigh of relief; it gave me the privilege of *not* taking everything on. I was 'permitted' to focus on two key behaviours that needed to change. It was like a huge load that had been taken off and this compelled me to keep coming back.

When we had presentations, for example, from specialist speakers about sexual exploitation, the 'grooming line' and CSE warning signs, I became more informed and realised how little I knew about this dark area of society and the dangers my daughter could be facing each time she went missing. I knew now that I had to keep learning so that I could reconnect with her after she had gone missing and returned.

Learning about the importance of having the right supporters (glossary, p87) throughout the journey was paramount for me, especially when some family members told me to give up on her; that she would not change the actions which put her at risk. As a result of my daughter's missing episodes and after resolving my feelings of shame, I was aware of the importance of having as many people as possible to help me when she went missing. My goddaughter was one of my supporters. On one of the occasions when my daughter went missing, I had informed her. Her husband later saw my daughter walking a dog. He spoke to her and took a photo to show me that she was okay. This proved to me that texting my main active supporters was crucial. This is called 'campaign texting' in NVR (glossary, p87).

We were given information about sexual health and various websites we could research, such as CEOP (Child Exploitation and Online Protection), and nshn.co.uk, which has helpful information about distractions that someone can try instead of self-harming. We even had the head of the MET police working with Child Sexual Exploitation speak with us. He allowed us to fire questions at him. He was a very humble man who openly shared the weaknesses and strengths within the police force.

The area of reconciliation gestures (glossary, p87) was difficult to digest for most parents/grandparents because they had until then been following a policy of not rewarding bad behaviour. I, however, was able to relate to this by directing my thoughts to how I would meet the needs of an infant child that had been difficult but needed a nappy change: the child still needed the comfort of the nappy change, even though their behaviour was difficult. I would leave my daughter small inexpensive gifts like a pack of underwear or send her a loving text message.

Active resistance (glossary, p87) was an area where I could become quite creative, coming up with ways to stop the offensive behaviour without force, whilst resisting my old habits of escalation. For example, for almost three weeks I kept the front and back door key with me every night so that my daughter could not sneak out, as she had done so many times before.

I will keep the front and back door key with me every night!

It was a real inconvenience to the whole family, but I wanted her to understand how much we wanted her at home and safe.

The most distressing part of the course came when I had to deal with my own struggles/traumas that affected the way I responded to my daughter and the other children, which was what I had to do when writing the self-announcement (glossary, p87). It included time to look back, see my mistakes, accept my past and how my past decisions influenced her and my life negatively, possibly leading her to make wrong choices for her own life, also forgiving myself and moving forward. It took a lot of soul-searching and being honest with myself to do this. This step took me forward to then identify my daughter's struggles and where the disconnections started and continued to break down. This was another painful but very necessary process for forgiveness of myself, my daughter and others, so that healing could take place. I cried many times during this time and occasionally I still do when giving my testimony to new parents, because it involves reliving the pain and fear. The 'Still face' video with Professor Edward Tronick[8] gives an insight into how a parent's reactions can affect the emotional development of a baby. The exercise that we did in relation to it was instrumental in helping me recognise how ignoring a child's needs could be extremely disturbing to the child and could make them feel rejected.

Learning to prepare for a 'Sit-in' (glossary, p87) was a very empowering experience because it allowed me to gain back the strength to be a better parent by being able to speak to my daughter about her behaviours from my 'small basket', which I would not tolerate.

My sit in was slightly altered. I did a 'lie-in' on one night that she went missing – I stayed awake laying in her bed, phoning and texting her until she came home at 6am. She was shocked to see me there. It helped her realise how important she was to me. Instead of my past chastisement, when she went missing I used my NVR principles and welcomed her home. I was happy she was home safely; that was the priority, and I was glad I had NVR to help me with this attitude.

The course ended with a reminder to look after ourselves (glossary, p87). I, for example, enjoyed swimming. So, I started taking time to do that, as well as losing a few pounds. We had a wonderful graduation ceremony, which my daughter and two of my other children attended. I received a certificate and believed the journey was close to finishing, but, like my daughter's unexpected early birth, there was more surprises in store for me. She did have one last missing episode after the course, but I knew what to do and to say when she returned.

After completing the NVR specialist group sessions in March 2015, I subsequently attended more than three separate training sessions. These training courses were offered to professionals who worked within the CAMHS or social care field. As a result, I was exposed to their work limitations and challenges. I had been very angry with 'professionals'

8 The still face experiment was first developed by Dr Edward Tronick in 1975. We regularly use his brief YouTube film about this experiment and then ask participants to try it out in pairs to demonstrate the NVR concepts of connection, brief disconnection and long-term disconnection to get away from Tronick's description of 'the good, the bad and the ugly', which we find too judgemental. We also want to demonstrate with the exercise that even a brief disconnection of one minute is experienced as disturbing by parents and professionals alike, thereby showing that disconnections and moving out of contact is upsetting at any age in life, not just for an infant.

who, I felt, had made choices that did *not* help my daughter. She had been referred to CAMHS on at least three occasions and was refused. I therefore had a lot of negative thoughts towards this service. However, due to training alongside professionals, I got an appreciation and respect for their frustration and the restrictions that they had to adhere to. There were funding cuts and priorities in providing services which often prevented them from helping.

I did not expect that: what had started as the nightmare experience of my child going missing, was leading me to learn more about, and work with, professionals.

While I had previously had little respect for them, I now developed a better understanding for their perspective. I also co-facilitated a specialist NVR group, which involved 14 weekly sessions and a café visit, and included four supervision meetings with a family therapist. Each session had pre-meetings about the areas of NVR that we would discuss during that evening. The sessions were always followed by up to an hour of debriefing, which allowed us to reflect on how the session went and to discuss issues that had come up, which were all documented. The debrief minutes would then be typed up and distributed for further reflection and used as preparation for the following week's session.

I did not know what to expect from the 'supervision' meetings, but I realised that they were scheduled strategically throughout the course to support the facilitators. These two-hour meetings were set aside for us to work through and discuss any issues that had come up while running the course. A steering group of stakeholders also offered us support and advice while the group was running.

I have since trained to get NVR level 1 and 2/3 certificates, as well as an NVR peer mentoring certificate. I also co-facilitated NVR training sessions for professionals and parent groups in nine areas in the UK. Additionally, I attended and presented at the international and national NVR conferences in Sweden, Germany, London and most recently in Southampton. I developed my own acronym for the key NVR parental values, 'CAARERS', which stands for **C**onnection, **A**spiration, **A**bilities, **R**esponsibilities, **E**ducation, **R**espect and **S**afety. I believe that parents hold on to every word of the graduate parent testimonies with the hope that they too will find solutions to the personal challenges they are experiencing with their child or children. One mum said, 'If *you* could get through *your* challenges using NVR, then I could use it to help with *my* situation with *my* son as well'. Parents are given hope for their circumstances, while many professionals develop empathy to share with their colleagues and parents they work with. For some of them, however, I believe parent participation is still looked upon just as another therapeutic technique.

I cannot end without mentioning a parent group that I was recently helping to co-facilitate: we had an unusually high number of fathers attending right to the end. These six fathers came from various backgrounds. I was overwhelmed to see their level of engagement, to the point that two of the fathers were getting their child to learn and practice some of the NVR principles while they were still on the course. It was a fantastic extension of their learning and engagement with their child. One father told us that he realised he was a different person before NVR and that he wished he had learned about NVR before he had his children. Another father said that my testimony really helped him connect with NVR, because of me stressing the importance of 'responding' and not 'reacting', which was empowering for him. His relationship with his ex-wife, who also attended the group, changed before our eyes from a silent, distant and cold one to a warm, friendly and compatible one. I also came to understand that our NVR graduate parent testimonies, spoken with genuine passion, are tangible, extendable and relatable, and hence powerful, and have a huge impact on parents and professionals alike, which makes a tremendous contribution to NVR.

Lastly, I want to revisit a recent conversation that I had with my husband. He was my main active supporter but unfortunately he was never able to attend the NVR parent group due to our childcare circumstances. He led me to understand that in his native language, Twi, from Ghana, there is no word that translates directly to the English word 'empathy'. He therefore never truly understood its definition until I explained and demonstrated the word to him. I described how people can relate to others better by thinking about what it would be like to step into their shoes during the experience. I described the emotional impact of doing that: arousing compassion for the person they are relating to. It was a real revelation for me that other people may also not have a clear understanding of this powerful emotional experience, which is so important throughout the NVR journey[9].

Finally, I am due to start co-facilitating two more new groups this year. My daughter has now moved into her own flat, and we are in contact with each other regularly. I know she is much safer now. She knows we love her and we are always there for her. NVR did not solve all my issues with

9 The Whorf - Sapir Hypothesis is the theory of linguistic relativity, demonstrated with examples of the language of the Hopi who have no concept of past tenses and who, so the representatives of this theory think, cannot understand the concepts of physics. These ideas were developed by Edward Sapir and later extended by his student Benjamin Whorf. The theory concludes that human languages determine the structure of the real world rather than vice versa, and that this structure is different from one language to another.
We do not concur with this hypothesis. In Deborah's example, while the Twi language does not contain a word for 'empathy', she explains how she still succeeded with her examples and explanations and was able to give her husband a good lived experience of the concept behind the word. We believe that he will now be able to explain and demonstrate it to another native Twi speaker.

my daughter but it enabled me to have tools to move forward and brush away all the things that had buried my hope. My spirit is restored to help me support my husband, my daughter, my other children and others in the wider community. Like a person who wants to bake a cake, you need the ingredients: the bowl, the mixing spoon, the baking pan and the oven, but until you get the tools and learn how to use them, you will not be able to bake the cake. NVR, along with my faith, has given me the tools I needed to resurrect my buried hope. The journey continues, because NVR is a lifestyle that needs to be practiced for it to become part of your daily choices.

The circle of hope in parent participation is:

New parents move from helplessness and hopelessness by feeling **inspired** and **encouraged** by the graduate parents' stories and examples and how the NVR principles helped them to overcome suffering and pain.

Louise's story and participation in NVR

Our family consists of me (Louise), my husband, my daughter from a previous marriage, and our daughter, who was born 10 years later. At the age of six, our youngest was diagnosed with high functioning autism after having trouble at school. She was refusing to co-operate and showing no respect for the teachers. I now know that her behaviour was classic, but then neither I nor the school understood. We were referred to our local Child and Adolescent Mental Health Service (CAMHS), and my husband and I attended a few sessions of one-to-one NVR. Due to work commitments, my husband could not attend all the sessions on offer. Although we found some of the ideas controversial, such as no punishment, we did learn about de-escalation. Together with learning more about autism and changing her school, we got through the primary school years.

When she went to secondary school, life became very difficult again. My eldest daughter returned home from university, and when her younger sister attacked her, it was time to seek help. Again, we were referred to CAMHS. This time, it was suggested that we attend an NVR group course, where most of the parents were struggling to cope with children who had ASD and other diagnoses. So, in September 2012, I joined a group of about 12 families and a couple of people who had already done the course and who were sharing with us the benefits of attending the group (these were graduate parents). Straight away I felt it was somewhere I could be open and honest about our difficulties, as there were plenty of others with far greater problems. The group was very diverse. People from every walk of life. Professional people with plenty of money, people who were not working or unable to work and who found money a struggle, people who could read and some who could not. They were all working together to improve their family lives.

My husband still could not attend every week, however he was doing shift work so he did attend a few of the sessions.

The first week was familiar. We were taught about de-escalation (glossary, p87). There was a lot of resistance in the group – I think all of us found it hard to accept that we played a part in our child's behaviour. The graduate parents explained that they too found it hard to accept that the parenting techniques that they had used before on their older children simply did not work for every child. Sometimes we must use different techniques for different children. That really resonated with me. It was the real-life stories of real situations of the graduate parents that inspired me to keep attending. They were genuine people, who were going through similar problems, who had attended the course and were willing to share their experiences, both their successes and their failures, because they believed that it was helping. It was their involvement and the lack of judgement that kept me attending week after week. No-one was ever made to feel like a bad parent.

Our homework for the first week was to simply notice when our children 'kicked off'. What had happened just before the outburst? What had we said or done? What else was going on at the time? Could we have done something different that might have changed the outcome?

The following week, we all reported back to the group. Even after just one week we all felt like one group – facilitators, graduate parents and new families all working together. Some parents found it hard to answer some of the questions but were happy to describe incidents that had occurred. Gradually, some people could see that they might have been able to do something differently. We even had the opportunity to re-enact a situation and practise what we would have liked to have done and what we could do if the same situation should arise again in the future. I could see that sometimes my husband might say things sharply and with a disapproving expression on his face. This was usually followed by an outburst of some description from our daughter, which inevitably escalated the situation. When I discussed this with him, he informed me that I often did not help matters either!

We talked about 'Striking when the iron is cold'. These concepts were not new to us, as we had both had the one-to-one sessions before. We agreed that we would keep an eye on each other and just say 'NVR' or raise a hand, when we noticed the other was not being helpful. We tried to keep it light-hearted and treat it almost like a game. The following week, life was much improved. Our daughter did not even seem to notice our secret signs or comments to each other. We did not need to say it often, as we were more aware of our own behaviour. We noticed that my husband usually got the brunt of her temper. He would stand still and let her push against him, both physically and metaphorically. I think she thought of him as an invincible punchbag. He started to walk away, crumple if hit and look hurt instead of angry. At first, she got cross with him. She could not understand that she could hurt him. Then she became upset that she might hurt him. Between him moving out of the way and her realising that she can hurt him, the violence reduced considerably.

The word 'no' was often a trigger point. We learnt to say: 'Not now'. For example, she loves biscuits. Often before dinner, she would ask to raid the biscuit tin. I started to say things like: 'Dinner will be ready very soon' or, 'After dinner, you may have some chocolate biscuits,' or, 'You may even have some ice cream with them, if you wish'. We became quite expert at rewording to avoid the word 'no'. 'Can I stay up and watch TV?' Reply: 'Your bedtime is…' or, 'It's important for your health that you have enough sleep' or, 'I care that you get enough sleep because I love you'. If she wanted me to do something and I did not want to or could not do it, I might tell her what I was prepared to do instead. When she said: 'Mummy, I want you to stay with me until I fall asleep', I would tell her that I would stay with her and help her to relax with a short meditation, then I would leave her to fall asleep. We were learning to negotiate.

One of the lasting memories I have is standing in the playground waiting for my daughter to come out of primary school and watching other mothers greeting their children. Their children would run out of school to their mothers and give them a hug. They were both pleased to see each other. Mothers would reach into their pockets and pull out a treat; a small bar of chocolate, a packet of crisps or a hairband. One girl even used to ask her mother if she had had a good day. I did think this was probably exceptional. However, my child was usually last out and in a bad mood. I was more often greeted with a kick if I was not dragging her out from under the desk. On the way home, she would moan. It made me very depressed. In the end, I said that she could moan at me for half the journey and that for the rest of the walk home, we must try and find something positive to talk about. Silence reigned but it was better than moaning. I felt so envious of the other parents. I do not think I even liked my child. When I have spoken about this in a group as a graduate parent, I have discovered that other parents can relate to loving their child but not always liking them. It allows them to discuss their negative feelings. By breaking the silence and speaking of our hurts (glossary, page 87), it allows us to be honest with ourselves and helps us to heal.

The second NVR skill we were taught was reconciliation gestures (glossary, p87). As the name suggests, they can be a way of making up and saying sorry when things have gone wrong, but they can be so much more. They are small acts of loving kindness. After my experience in the school playground I could not wait to put this into practise. On the way home from the session, I stopped and bought a small bar of chocolate. I was concerned that my effort may be rejected. We had been warned by the facilitator that this often happens. The child may not feel that they deserve it, or they do not trust that it has been given unconditionally. However, I left it on her pillow with a note saying that we both love her. When she found it, she asked what it was all about, and I said that I did not think I had told her recently that I loved her. She agreed that I had not and ate the chocolate. I did not get a 'thank you' but I did not get it thrown at me either. I felt so much better at being able to do something nice for my daughter. It was not a reward, it was 'just because' I loved her. This was something I had been wanting to do for years but had been afraid that it might be seen as a reward for bad behaviour. Gradually, I felt able to do more acts of loving kindness. I realised that it was not about her response but about how much better I felt being kind. It helped me to see that I did love her.

On one occasion, I knew things were not going so well at school with her friends so I bought some lace knickers in the sales. There were two bra-and-pant sets. I gave the bras to my older daughter and the knickers to the younger. The reaction of the oldest daughter was amazing. By now she was working. I suppose I had stopped buying her unexpected gifts. This shows that you can still treat all the children equally even if you are 'doing NVR' on one child only. This is an example that I often tell in groups, when people ask what they should do when a sibling starts to show signs of jealousy. The NVR tools can be used for every child and adapted to their needs. Everyone likes an unexpected show of affection, a bunch of flowers, a cup of tea, a kiss on the cheek from a loved one.

As mentioned, the youngest was having trouble at school. One day, she refused to go. This was a first for me. Luckily, we had nearly finished the course. So, now I had quite a few skills under my belt. Making use of our family values, baskets, supporters and advanced communication skills, I succeeded in getting her to agree to go to school in the morning break. By lunchtime, I was called in for a discussion with the deputy head. We had a frank and open discussion, where I explained that I had been attending an NVR group. He asked what I was going to do when she got home from school. I said that I would make a cake and see how it went from there. He seemed to think that this was a very novel approach but agreed that cake would make him feel better, too.

On my return home, I made a lemon meringue pie; her favourite. At 4pm she walked in through the door and slammed the door shut. She threw her bag in the hall and kicked her shoes off up the wall. I stood in the kitchen shaking. I called to her in the calmest, happiest voice I could find and said: 'Hello, I bet you are glad to be home. Come and look in the oven.' She came into the kitchen. 'I have made this especially for you. I thought it might cheer you up after a bad day!' We shared it for dessert. She was as pleased as punch. 'Thanks, mum,' she said. 'Yes, it was a horrid day. I do not want another one like that! Can I talk to you after I have taken this horrid uniform off?'

'I have made this especially for you. I thought it might cheer you up after a bad day'. She was pleased as punch.

The power of pudding! I used this example not only to show that doing something nice after a bad day does not reward the behaviour but that the gesture can be shared, as the child still knows it was done with them in mind. I remember that one family, after having learnt about reconciliation gestures, bought their daughter a whole salmon and put it in the fridge for the child's sole consumption. The rest of the family were furious. This did appear to them to be rewarding bad behaviour. Instead of uniting, it caused a rift in the family. After listening to my story, they said that in future they would try to let the young person know that, although they were going to share the salmon, it was bought because they knew it was her favourite. Some weeks later they reported back to the group that they had all gone to the cinema as a family but had told the young person that she could choose what they went to see. This apparently worked very well, and the daughter really appreciated that she chose the family outing.

As I have mentioned, my husband was only able to attend a few sessions during the course. However, it helped enormously. It was not me coming home from the sessions, telling him how we should change our parenting, but him asking what I had learned and how we could put it into practice.

One of the sessions, which he attended alone, was about writing an announcement. He also participated in the practice group, playing the part of our daughter having the announcement read to her. By all accounts he played her very well! Apart from being the topic of conversation the following week, it really helped him to feel what it was like to be our daughter.

He has continued to practise NVR and keeps me in check when I forget to use it. Our daughter is now 19 and has just finished studying music at college. One morning last year, she had been particularly awkward. She had been quite rude to me and I was not feeling very loving towards her. She then demanded that I take her to college, refusing to carry her bass guitar on the bus. I refused but my husband said he would take her. I was really cross with him. Why was he going to take her to college when she has a free bus pass and she had been so rude? He waited until she was out of the room and reminded me that he was 'doing NVR'.

Our daughter attained her grade eight singing certificate with distinction and is starting university in September, where she will be living independently away from home. We could not be prouder.

Since becoming a graduate parent, I have spoken at a conference in Germany. It was amazing how many professional people wanted to talk to me to hear my story and my experiences of using NVR. I also trained as a peer mentor to help train future graduate parents. When parents first start to share their experiences, it is hard to know what to say and how to say it. It is a great honour to be able to help them to find their own voice and see them helping others. I also assist on training courses that train professionals in the NVR skills and support them to facilitate the NVR courses. It always surprises me that, with all their knowledge, education and experience, they want to listen to me. I am currently involved in writing a training programme for volunteer parents, from their starting point to onward support during their life as a volunteer.

Louise's husband's perspective

We had been struggling as a family for several years. We had tried various methods to improve things and help our daughter to cope with life. We thought that we had lost control and no amount of discipline or punishment appeared to make any difference. I was reluctant to join a group and share our problems with professionals, let alone strangers. I was fearful of being judged and criticised. However, I realised that we needed some help and if this was all there was, we had better give it a try.

We both attended the first few weeks, as it fitted in with my work roster. When I could not attend, Louise always returned home with new ideas that

I was willing to try. I was sceptical that they would work but she seemed quite keen. I was surprised by how quickly we saw a change. It was also hard for me to accept that occasionally *we* contributed to the outbursts, and that we must look to ourselves to make the change.

I was pleased to find that I was not the only man there[10]. Anything to do with the children had always been a female domain. I was made to feel very welcome by a man who was a graduate parent who had a son who also had autism. Knowing that he would be there every week and that I would not be the only man helped me to return in the future. The sessions continued through the half-term holiday. So Louise stayed with our daughter and I attended the session alone. I remember participating in a role play in which I played the role of my daughter. I dreaded it – I have always hated roleplays. I decided that the only way I was going to survive this ordeal was to throw myself into it. I soon had the rest of the group laughing. It was good to be able to see the situation from a different perspective. Yes, it did look funny, but I found out what it felt like to be my daughter. She was scared, frustrated and angry, because she did not understand what was happening. She did not understand facial expressions or tones of voice. I learned that we need to not show our frustrations. We need to remain calm to enable her to hear what we are saying. We need to make sure we have her attention before we speak; it is less frustrating for everyone.

Even on the occasions that I could not attend, I found that I was keen to learn from Louise on her return what had happened in the session. I felt it brought us closer together, as we were working as a team. In the past, I felt that she was telling me how to be a father and that I was doing it all wrong. This inevitably caused tension between us, which rubbed off on to our girls. NVR has helped our family communicate in a more productive fashion. I have even found myself using NVR at work.

10 Naama Gershy and Haim Omer, as well as Julia Jude and Veronica Rivera-Gould, write about the challenges, possibilities and benefits of including fathers in NVR work.

Part 3: Discussion of commonalities and differences

Family status of the three parents, particularly in relation to fathers in the three families

While Sara was a single mum with a non-residential partner, Louise and Deborah were both with husbands during their first NVR groups. Due to work commitments, Louise's husband attended about a third of the 12 NVR sessions. He was, however, fully engaged, reminding her of the NVR skills when she felt low. Because he attended some sessions with her together, he was open to discussions and found it easier to understand the context and setting. He was far more engaged with the process, more so than with earlier therapy sessions that Louise had attended on her own. During these therapy sessions he stayed disengaged and was not part of it. But he felt included in the NVR group and in applying the principles to family life, even when he could not attend. Prior to the group, it had been Louise's job to look after the children. There were even two sessions which he attended on his own. He liked the fact that the roles were reversed, and he could tell Louise what he had learned. At one stage in their life before attending the NVR group, they had been to family therapy together, but if anything, family therapy had put him off therapy altogether. He felt judged and blamed because the emphasis was on him. In NVR, the emphasis was on their parenting together, and he experienced no blame or judgement. That enabled him to stay involved.

In Deborah's case, her husband enabled her to participate in the group, with him staying behind and looking after the children. Although Deborah shared everything as much as possible, it did not allow him to have a full understanding of the NVR concepts as a lived experience in the group. This therefore led to disagreements about how to raise the children and created difficulties. Even though he accepted that this new way of parenting may be useful, he resisted the ideas. For example, he did not want to wait until 'the iron is cold', but to deal with a situation straight away, until it was resolved. Deborah felt unsupported, and that he acted at times like what Uri Weinblatt[11] called an 'active adversary' even though he did not mean to challenge her. It distinguished between different types of supporters that parents should look at when choosing who they invite into the caring community around

11 This description refers to a handout from a workshop with Uri Weinblatt, Margate, 2007.

their family. Some people who present themselves as supporters can be 'adversaries', who do not have the best interests of the parent or the child at heart and may undermine the parent's parental presence. Weinblatt suggested that the best that can be done with these types of so-called 'supporters', is to put them into the position of a 'neutral' person, while he proposed that an initially neutral person can become an active supporter, if circumstances allow.

Weinblatt's take on supporters helped us to understand why it made processing the NVR skills and adapting them to family life a great deal harder for Deborah, because she knew that she also had to win her husband into this. Over time he has accumulated enough knowledge about NVR so that he sometimes reminds Deborah of the skills when old patterns creep in.

Deborah's husband had turned up a few times during group sessions and professional training in order to give her something. He saw the setting and the people and was even on one occasion asked to say a couple of things about fathers from his perspective. He liked that, and he felt afterwards more included and accepted things more when they discussed NVR at home.

Deborah still believes that it would have made a huge difference had they attended together, because then he would have understood that Deborah was not trying to 'manipulate' him to change, but change would have come naturally to him as part of the NVR process. Not coming allowed him to stay in his comfort zone. They could have alternated attending like Louise and her husband, but Deborah's husband preferred the childcare support over attending the meetings, which, in his eyes, might have made him question his parenting skills much more than Deborah could have done on her own. Deborah still felt that his was a positive support, because she could go home and off-load, and he was willing to learn about NVR, without wanting to apply it himself and give it a chance to transform himself, as she saw it did to other fathers in the groups.

In Sarah's situation, her partner would drop her at the sessions. She did not share anything about it with him, as she still felt embarrassed about her home situation. She also initially noticed attending couples bickering with each other, leaving her feeling relieved that she could make her own choices at home in her own time. She needed her partner for escapism, to get away from the dire reality. For her, it was good enough that he offered lifts. Only when her son got involved with gangs did she tell him, because there were visible signs of destruction to her front door which he noticed. When he asked her about it and she told him about her son's concerning behaviour, he immediately offered to repair and paint it. He also shared with her that he had been a troubled teenager, too, and that it was good that she did not judge her son. Although he was supportive in this way, Sarah kept him apart from further involvement and instead chose her mum as her main supporter.

She wanted to keep her special time (her 'me-time') with the partner separate, thus denying herself the opportunity of having him as a strong ally and supporter.

Comparing these experiences in relation to the attending of partners, we feel that parents have a much smoother transition to applying NVR consistently if their partners and main supporters attend at least some part of the sessions.

When a man attends without their partner, as experienced by Deborah in one of the groups she co-facilitated, he could be more himself, showing his emotional connection with his son, without being judged by the wife. In this case, the family attended family therapy sessions alongside the course, and the therapist reported that the wife 'ridiculed' her husband. She even told the therapist that she felt 'embarrassed' by him. He said in the NVR session that he felt 'inadequate' around her, crying when talking about this. He also realised that he had put down his son. When moving forward in the process, he went on an outing of football with his son, during which the boy fell into a hole. He had wandered off during the match. When he could not get out of this hole by himself, he phoned his dad. Several days before this episode, the son had lost his phone at home and the father had stayed calm and had helped him to find it. When he talked about this incident to the group, everyone was moved, as this phone had later helped the son to get out of the hole, possibly saving both father and son hours of distress. After this incident, the same father told the group that he feels he is now a 'better person' and that his relationship with his son has improved tremendously. They now do DIY together. Unfortunately, we do not know anything about his wife's current views on him and on his transition. We expect that her opinion of him now may have changed as a ripple effect. A risk stays anyway: Partners who do not attend can often feel left behind, even to the point of marriage breakdown.

This incident evidences that men are just as capable of benefitting from NVR, applying the skills and questioning their own parenting and values as women are. Practising NVR together in the home as a couple seems to be the preferred version. Parents who attend on their own without a partner embracing it had to be much more resilient and determined, because they still had to face the old patterns and habits in their partners.

Supporters

NVR made Sarah and her mum aware her parental presence (glossary, p87) over time had been lost by family members undermining her in front of her children, as they made her feel in front of them that she was inadequate in her ability to be a positive parent in their lives. She realised that she, too, contributed to this by always going to her mum for a second opinion in the past, like most daughters do. Instead of having confidence in themselves to decide what form of action to take and use their own judgement towards their child's unacceptable behaviours. They see their own parents as wiser than themselves.

Each of the supporter positions in the preceding chapter is equally valid. In NVR, we appreciate support in whatever form it is given. However, we do not believe that anything that undermines the self-determination and parental presence of the parent should be called 'supportive', even if the *intention* is to be supportive. Our formula about support is therefore 'only support which is experienced as support is support'. Having strengthened her parental presence at home, Sarah is now able to point out to others when she feels undermined by them, because she realises the negative impact on her parental presence. As a result, family members have now become real supporters in the NVR sense. They accept their time and place as supporters. The big learning point for us about supporters is that they are equally vigilant about the child as about the parent, in the sense how Haim Omer (Omer, 2017) describes vigilance. This prevents parental presence being lost again and parents becoming invisible to their child or to others as their parent.

Effects and impact on siblings

Sarah's daughter drew pictures for our second parent booklet (Heismann *et al*, 2013) with testimonies from parents, carers, family members, young people, their siblings and supporters. This experience contributed enormously to building her confidence. She had been diagnosed with learning difficulties and experienced a lot of verbal and physical violence from her brother, as Sarah described earlier.

When her brother called his sister 'retard' and told her, 'You are a special girl because you have something wrong with you', she always felt intimidated and kept herself to herself far away from him, clinging to her mother at all times. She would never stay alone with her brother, not for even five minutes. His behaviour towards her undermined her low self-esteem even further. She would say to Sarah, 'Why do you allow him to hit me and not do anything about it?', which made Sarah feel worse and more unable to protect her daughter from her son. As her daughter was not good at communicating verbally, she started to express her feelings and her suffering by drawing pictures, which were published in the second parent book in 2013.

Sarah used some of the NVR concepts, mainly de-escalation and reconciliation gestures (glossary, p87), to improve the relationship between her children at home. They would sit down for a movie night at home with chocolates, taking turns to choose which film to watch. Sarah also got her son to repair things for his sister. She would ask her daughter to choose chocolates for her brother in the shop to give to him. When they had a bad day with each other, Sarah would remind her daughter of the nice things he had done for her and with her. Gradually, she started to stay with him on her own and develop trust in him.

Deborah's children were initially very anxious when their sister went missing, but afterwards became very angry with her and thought that she acted selfishly.

Deborah had to help them to overcome their anger and explain and model to them the NVR approach of connection before correction. That was sometimes very hard for them to understand.

Louise's older daughter became one of her main supporters after she left home. When things happened at home, Louise composed text messages for her, which she could then send to her sister as if they came from her. She later also made a video about NVR for her school, where she worked as a teacher to demonstrate how she used the skills in her classroom.

When we are running our parent groups, people are often coming back saying that NVR has created more sibling rivalry, if they did not include their other children in what they were doing. We then have to explain to them that it is crucial that all the NVR principles and skills are used with the whole family, even though we concentrate on one child at a time. Siblings can really help with the process when they are included, just as Louise did with her older daughter and Sarah with her younger daughter, although the latter did not know anything about NVR at that point. Sometimes the suffering of the siblings is not appreciated or even seen by the parents. In Deborah's case, it took a long time to overcome the resentment and for the healing and forgiveness to take place, because the other children felt that they had lost their family home due to their sister's behaviour.

In order to help parents talk to their children, we created a siblings leaflet after a booster session that we had held with siblings. This leaflet explains the NVR principles in a simple language and is given to parents to use when talking to younger brothers and sisters.

We also organised a picnic with siblings, where they could relate to each other. We always invite siblings and other family members to our graduation ceremonies at the end of the 12-week sessions. We collected siblings' testimonies for our second parent booklet. All these materials can help brothers and sisters to see that, sometimes, they also contribute to the escalation at home. They are often 'parentified' and take on their parents' responsibility, which they find hard to step out of. Adjustments have to be made by everyone in the family, including any brothers or sisters.

Persistence in NVR

The sequence of using the skills and principles, or the clumsiness with which they are employed when using them, is not important. It is the determination to keep doing NVR, staying persistent in the use of the skills, no matter how it is received.

What counts is what works best for the individual child and parent, regardless of gender, age, disability.

NVR is about attending to the relationship for both parent and child, making connections which have not been made before, listening to each other's needs and hurts and respecting each other's positions. As a result, it improves the mental health of both.

Families can enjoy what they fought so hard for: a loving relationship, where each other's presence is celebrated. In our cases, the children, who had given all three mothers so much grief before, are now their parents' best friends and supporters, and a source of great pride. All three still have moments where they do not get on with their children, but they can now hold on to hope and enjoy what they have built together, regardless of their troubles, past and present.

The impact on young people

In the cases of all three authors, the young people have changed, regardless of their gender and age. This is not only due to maturation, but to the persistent application of the skills, particularly nurturing and prioritising the relationship and showing parental presence.

All of our children are now working or studying, which we had never expected them to be doing. They are more emphatic and supportive with their siblings and parents, and more helpful, even though they never attended a single session themselves.

Initially all three of us did not tell our children about NVR and what we were doing during the meetings for fear that they would use it against us, as Sarah's son had done during the family therapy sessions that they had previously attended.

Gradually, the children picked up that we did something different and realised that this made an impact on their lives together and how they related to them. Some even asked their parent in an argument when they would go back to NVR, because it seemed to help them. Louise's daughter told her that 'the parent classes seem to work, and she is a better parent now'. All three children realised and appreciated that their parents had made the effort because of them, despite them being difficult. When initially they felt blamed, they relaxed that thought, when the parents managed to tell them that it was not about blaming them or singling them out, but about their relationship with each other and about how they can get on better with each other and be better parents to their children.

Deborah's daughter said in the graduation ceremony at the end of the specialist group that Deborah had attended: 'I see that my mum has changed'. She saw that, instead of escalating when things were difficult, her mum now responded with love and understanding, even encouraging her siblings to forgive her. Unconditional love is not easy. It is much easier to tell your child, 'You are now old enough to sort yourself out', and even throw the young person out of the home. What NVR does, is help parents to become an anchor, and for their home to become a safe haven, which then can give rise to a calm child. When parents are no longer responding in the expected harmful patterns, the young person can stop in their tracks. Initially they might become confused. As we see it, it puts space between the old unhelpful patterns and new ones, allowing everyone to calm down. This way, NVR has a ripple effect for the young person even if they are not directly involved in the sessions. We see this positive effect again and again: if one part of the system changes what they are doing, it has a knock-on effect on everyone else. As we see it, the young person does not need to know what their parent has learned, as long as they get the positive results.

Shame

We agreed that shame is an important feeling that had held the negative patterns in the three families in place. In order to compare the impact of shame, we need to go back to each of the three family cases and hear how shame has affected them: shame was an inevitable part of Deborah's NVR journey, because, as mentioned earlier in this book, her daughter went missing at least 32 times and on most of these occasions the police came to her home to ask questions, and even one time checked under her bed to see if she was there. The shame of having neighbours wondering why the police were yet again at the home was embarrassing for the whole family, and each time not knowing whether she would come back safely was emotionally and physically draining. The frequency was such that her youngest son became so comfortable with the police that he would try to take their handcuffs to play with them. The family went from shame to fear and back again over a period of several years. It was the worst rollercoaster ride Deborah could ever imagine.

Learning more about the risks her daughter was putting herself in each time she went missing only escalated Deborah's desire to push the shame away and focus on getting as much help from as many people she could trust to share with when her daughter went missing. The shame that initially held her from exposing her daughter's times of departure was something she lived with for a while, but eventually she realised that remaining silent would and could end up causing more harm to her daughter rather than helping her. Deborah recalled having to tell her own mother and experiencing deep shame and feeling like a failure that she was not able to keep her daughter safe at home. Even though it was not said out loud, she felt these thoughts were in the back of family members' and friends' minds.

Deborah did her best not to allow shame to dominate her thoughts, though. It was not an easy battle. On one occasion, when her daughter had gone missing, they had contacted the police and it had been reported that she had been seen locally. The police then requested that Deborah should come with them to help identify her. She was pregnant at the time and did not want to go alone. So she went with her eldest daughter. They both had to get in the back of the police car. Deborah felt so ashamed because she knew that, watching this, her neighbours would most likely think that she had done something wrong and was in trouble with the law. When the police car drove very fast, Deborah and her oldest daughter became so frightened that they held on to each other hoping they would not die. When they arrived where her younger daughter had been sighted, she had already gone. That day, she did not come home. Deborah and her eldest daughter will forever remember that horrifying experience.

However, this helped Deborah to see the importance of sharing the information about her daughter's missing episodes so more people could be looking out for her. She realised that the more people who knew when her daughter went missing, the more eyes and ears were able to look out for her. NVR helped her to work through the shame, break it down in order to move forward to help her daughter, herself and her family. There was a point when her eldest son would not speak with his younger sister for over a year. Deborah continued to encourage him to reconnect with her. She was able to reason with him that, if she, Deborah, could forgive her, then he should forgive her too. She got this message across to him because NVR had helped her to change her own attitude and behaviour towards her daughter. Later when she attended a conference on shame with Uri Weinblatt in May 2019, in London, she learned how shame can be regulated in and between individuals and families.

In Louise's family, she and her husband felt shameful about being unable to control the behaviour of their young child. They felt that they must be bad parents who were not able to teach their daughter the right way to behave. That led them to run around the house closing all the windows so that the neighbours could not hear what was going on when she went into a 'melt-down'. They also never admitted to the authorities, counsellors or the school, how bad things really were, because of fear that she might be taken away from them if they were deemed to be 'out-of-control' parents. If someone knocked on the door, her daughter would run and hide in her room.

If someone knocked on the door, she would run and hide in her room.

Louise now wonders whether her daughter may have picked up her parents' shame and fear of other people detecting their difficulties with her and planning to take her away from the family. Even now, she never wants her past behaviour referred to. Once she left secondary school, she changed her name, saying that she wanted to be a new person and start again. Louise's older daughter went through a period of such deep shame that she did not invite her friends home because she was worried that her sister might misbehave or say something to her friends which might upset them to the point that they would not want to stay her friend any more. When she was out with her in the street one day, for example, her sister commented about a stranger at the top of her voice: 'No wonder that he's so fat. Look what they are eating while walking in the street. Shall I go and tell them?' and Louise's daughter felt very embarrassed. On another occasion she had told her teacher that she 'stank'.

Sarah felt particularly ashamed when her house was raided by the police, which happened three times, and also when she had to go to court. She thought that professionals and neighbours would stereotype her as the typical lone-parent, who has no control over her son's criminal behaviour. Although nobody ever mentioned her family status, the fear that they might was always on her mind. Sarah became very anxious whenever she heard police sirens. This sound triggered her fear that they might be heading towards her house again. She kept her house spotless, just in case they would come and raid it again, constantly feeling stripped bare and violated.

The media and news add to shame, when parents are blamed for their children's criminal activities and become stereotyped in the statistics as 'deprived' families that create deviant behaviours. Even housing associations shame parents, when they threaten them with evictions. Parents never get away from shame.

In all three cases, the young person involved was also full of shame which led them to go into hiding or running away from home. They avoided the confrontation about their behaviour, even to the extent where it meant putting themselves at risk in the street, as Deborah's daughter did, rather than taking responsibility and saying sorry.

It took a long time for their parents to learn that they can support their children despite their difficult behaviour. All three parents could only do that after they had addressed their own deep-rooted feelings of shame, blame, guilt and fear, and forgiven themselves when writing their self-announcements. They had to realise first that they had allowed these negative feelings to prevent them from parenting in the way they would have liked to. Negative feelings had created negative relational patterns between them and their children, over which they had lost control. The self-announcement took the barriers down and allowed them to be honest with themselves and forgive themselves for the wrong decisions and choices that they had made in relation to their children.

Sarah could not do any form of sit-in because she felt that it could become confrontational and put the blame on her son, thus shaming him even further. When Deborah's daughter had missed many days in school, she had to face up to her shame when returning and face the comments from her teachers and peers, as well as the fact that she had got further and further behind with her work.

Louise's daughter was ashamed of her Asperger's diagnosis because it made her different – she felt stereotyped by others as socially inept and frustrated and angry.

She felt stereotyped by others as socially inept.

This demonstrates that shame is not located in one person in the family but passed around between family members. Shame needs to be addressed and can be regulated, as Uri Weinblatt shows in his workshop and books. Before doing NVR, the three parents did not know that it can be regulated.

They understood that they cannot stop their children pursuing their own lives and making their own decisions, even making mistakes. They also learned that parenting is not about enforcing their own desires on their children, but being persistent in their unconditional love for them and letting them know about it. This takes the burden of being responsible for their actions away, together with the shame. Instead, they had to let go of judgement, blame, guilt and shame and develop the anchoring strength to be there for them and use the concept 'connection before correction', even in their darker times.

When Deborah's daughter recently wrote an article about being homeless, Deborah acknowledged that she did not feel ashamed anymore and realised that she had moved on and had overcome it. While she had felt humiliated when others judged her in the past, she now felt proud that her daughter was able to share her story so creatively. Shame no longer had control of her. It was regulated, and she had learned to deal with it in herself, thereby freeing her daughter to regulate hers.

Summary of part 3

All three families moved from a 'You' position to a 'We' position, painfully looking at their own 'I' position in the process (Omer, 2010). Not one single person is the goal of the therapeutic process, but the dance and connection between them moving forward from a position of 'You' (the child) via 'I' (the parent) to a 'We' (Parent and child and supportive network, community).

While Haim Omer (2010) explains that NVR moves the parent from an 'I' to a 'We' position, in our work we have included a 'You' position as the first stage for most parents and families in the process of change, which is more in line with Martin Buber's 'It' (Buber, 2008)[12]. Parents usually totalise their children's challenging behaviours and cannot notice any exceptions when they first come to us. All positive aspects that they like or love have gone and they need to be re-connected to recover a sense of the child as a whole person again. We have shown that all people who are living in a household have to adjust their part in the previous often harmful patterns, including siblings, who also often carry the burden of shame and guilt. With the parents addressing their own feelings of guilt, blame, shame and fear and forgiving themselves and others for allowing them to maintain harmful patterns, the burden could gradually – sometimes quickly – be lifted, and unconditional love could allow new connecting patterns to arise over time. This process requires persistence, self-empathy, self-forgiveness and freedom of choice on the part of the parents, and support, love, empathy, compassion and solidarity on the part of others who accompany them in this process. Groups are an excellent place where these two parts can come together.

12 See also Martin Buber's 'I–Thou' as different from the 'I–It relationship.

Part 4: The contribution of parent participation to the NVR model

Values and beliefs about participation

We want to give new parents the self-belief and confidence to be their best and to achieve their own personal goals, just as we were able to do. That makes us feel good and gives us a sense of fulfilment, boosting our own self-esteem even further in a humble way. We have never walked out of an NVR parent group thinking, 'This was a very hard day' – we always leave on a high. We would not keep going back if we were not able to see how new parents and others manage to move forward and achieve their personal lightbulb moments. There is never a session where we don't learn something new and get something out of it.

Staying involved also keeps us on track. It is a two-way process. When new parents describe their lightbulb moment, we get excited and it has a domino effect. You can always leave every group feeling that it was good for someone. Our testimonies are not always the same. Hearing each other's testimonies again, we hear them differently each time, learning something new about the other graduate parent. Over time, it brings out a different angle and perspective. We go over our own experience again. Although we may have our own set-stories, something new comes up with every new parent. None of our testimonies are the same every time. We may say them with more emotion, a different body language, choose a different angle or description. If there is something that is relatable, we also give examples of other graduate parents, even though they may not be there.

We have created a shared store of NVR stories that we can tap into, even though the stories may not be our own. This archive now contains all NVR stories and experiences from our own lives and those of past groups and all parents we have come in touch with. Nothing gets lost, everything is validated and used for learning about human lived experience. These stories are stored in our minds and we can draw from them when needed and decide how we want to use them. This archive contains theory and practice and therefore provides a much richer and more accessible curriculum than many other parent courses may be able to offer. The knowledge that other people have practiced it and achieved good results keeps people believing and persisting, including ourselves.

In our experience, when testimonies are given, people are often thinking or even saying, 'My child isn't as bad as theirs, even though I've always believed that my situation is the worst in the world'. This experience is humbling. Even parents of children with different issues or diagnoses still feel that they can relate to these stories. Participation enables everyone to realise that they not alone and that support is offered at a time when many parents feel that they have little or no support.

We therefore believe that it is greatly important to have a number and a variety of graduate parents with stories that a wide diversity of people can relate to.

Our values and beliefs in relation to participation in the NVR parent groups require a non-judgemental attitude from each of us. At times, cultural backgrounds and the different 'social class' of other parents can be an issue to keep in mind. To be respectful of other opinions is important so that no ill-feelings between us and others occur.

Conditions that our presence and testimonies create

We believe that our participation creates an atmosphere of openness and learning. When graduate parents tell their stories, they make themselves vulnerable. By exposing our 'dirty laundry' in public, we 'disarm' the new parents. They are surprised that the graduate parents can do it, which makes what we are telling believable. There is a genuineness that comes across with our stories. Sharing our stories encourages the new parents to share theirs, but most times it is still painful for them. The new parents can put themselves in our shoes and show respect and empathy. This helps to put their own situation into perspective.

Because of our emotion and passion as story-tellers, it disarms judgement and competitiveness and opens the door for shared empathy and relationships on an equal level. Because empathy is aroused in the listener, they can then look at their own pain, directing and using this empathy to themselves. This enables new parents to develop a greater understanding of themselves. Showing someone else empathy allows the new parents to look at themselves and forgive themselves for the negative feelings about their child. Resonance (Rosa, 2019a; 2019b; Bauer, 2019) or a deep connection and relational bonding are developed, which allows new parents to open themselves up to the possibility of change in their own lives. Resonance is the dialogue, the call and response, where the response is not a mere echo. It is compared with the resonance that can be experienced in music with two guitars or two metronomes. Rosa (Rosa, 2019a, pp 37–47) describes four moments of resonance that are important:

1. The moment of affection.
2. The moment of self-effectivity, which is the moment of emotional connection and connectivity.
3. The moment of transformation, which allows a recipient to get affected and answer.
4. The moment of unavailability, which means that there are no guidelines how to achieve resonance in relationships, however hard we may try.

If it happens, the result and the means by which it happens are also not predictable. Even if we share stories of moments where resonance has taken place between graduate parents and new parents or between new parents, they cannot be automatically repeated or copied. They cannot be stored or increased or evidenced. These light bulb moments (Day, 2014), or 'Aha moments', when the penny drops, are part of the 'mystery' that Barnett Pearce (Pearce, 2007) so eloquently writes about. All these moments of resonance are unplanned and beyond our control. We hope that the experience of resonance has been transformative to the effect that it becomes a model for the subsequent dialogues with the child.

We nurture trust and a non-judgemental attitude during the whole process. This creates an openness that may not otherwise be present, thus enabling real learning and change to be achieved.

Our model and process of participation

If we are able to, we put ourselves forward during meetings. At other times we feel that others have more appropriate skills and experience to move things forward. Sometimes we step back, realising that we may need to access some further training or support. This process is running parallel with the invitation to participate. At times we feel compelled to participate because we have something to offer. At others, we can step back a little, because we know that there are others who can step in. That goes in line with our belief that new graduate parents should get the opportunity to have a voice, including new parents. If you continue talking, new parents may not feel prepared and encouraged to put themselves forward.

We also have to trust the professionals, because at the end of the day they run the courses. We have progressed enough to acknowledge and respect each participant's voice and knowledge and what they bring to the table. Knowing when to sit back and when it is not a good time to tell your story because someone else's story has to be heard is paramount for our participation. There is, therefore, also an element of self-restraint and mutual respect of the schedule and of the timing of things that guides us. Balancing this ensures that information and concepts can be delivered and new parents have enough time and space to absorb and reflect.

The reason why NVR is so convincing is – we think – that people can relate to the experiences that we share. The graduate parents provide an interactive, coloured illustration in a 3-D book of knowledge, which would otherwise be boring, dry and unreadable. We listen carefully to all the issues that are being raised and, if possible, use our own scenarios to demonstrate which NVR skills we have used in the past. This way, new parents may be able to adapt and relate what we have done to their own situation. We are not teaching something from a book, we are bringing our lived experience along.

Our testimonies bring NVR to life. We are speaking from the heart, which gives new parents a more detailed idea of how bad things were for our own families before NVR and how things have improved for us. This encourages them to continue attending the NVR Parent groups and wanting to learn more about the NVR principles and how to put the NVR tools into practice in their own homes.

We take time to listen to the new parents, support them during times of difficulty with their child and show them empathy and support, looking at and pointing out how far they have come and exploring ways out of their negative situations, particularly when some parents feel that they have slipped back two steps that week instead of going one step forward.

What we are bringing to participation

We are bringing our individual stories and experiences, which have molded our lives and which new parents admire.

We would like to think that we bring kindness to the group, lift participants' spirits when they are feeling a bit low, approach others with honesty, openness and a caring nature. We inspire new parents by sharing different examples of how we use the NVR tools, which then gives them new ideas. We enjoy being supportive and always go out of our way to be there if someone requires an extra chat after the session.

Through sharing our experiences, we have developed compassion and empathy for other parents and professionals. We would like them to fully understand what we have gone through ourselves with the hope that they can help themselves and their families. We do not want to tell our stories just for the sake of good story-telling and for others to admire our story-telling skills. Our desire is for it to have a positive impact on their lives. We are hoping that the learning about and through us brings about changes in their outlook, relationships and behaviours. We may all have different and horrific stories, but it is the little changes that we made in our lives that have made a difference, for example when using reconciliation gestures.

These little steps can give new parents hope: the small adjustments that are achievable and sustainable rather than radical, big steps.

Parents are quick to notice the negatives, but do not notice the little positive things that happen and that we see as stepping stones towards connection before correction. If we make them to look harder, they will also see the positives. Sometimes we point out when small changes have already occurred, and the parents have not even noticed. For example, Sarah once said to a parent who had complained about her child's disrespectful behaviour but afterwards mentioned that the same child had made her a cup of tea: 'See what happened today? Your child didn't have to make you a cup of tea, but she chose to do it. That is positive!' And that to us is a ray of hope. We always think that tiny steps are the way forward.

We can help them to celebrate achievements, however little they may be, which slowly builds their self-esteem and self-efficiency. We listen carefully when people share their home dramas and interrupt them to bring their awareness to seeing things from the rainbow basket perspective (glossary, p87). We tease out all the small things in their child that they may have disconnected from. We also draw out their hidden strengths and self-efficacy, bring it to the forefront and highlight them as stepping stones to re-connect with their child.

Stories of failure have as much significance for us as stories of success, because they prove that there is no perfect parent. We make parenting attainable. We sometimes say: 'Life is not perfect, but it is a lot better than it was before.' If we continue to fight and strive for the perfect self, child and parenting, we are bound to fail, disconnect and lose everything. We hold on to the little steps in order to reach the ultimate goal of reconnecting with our children. The behaviour may well continue, but the positive development within the relationships allows us to remain aligned with our children and receptive to them.

Before, we had not been receptive to each other. We believe that, once people build some mutual respect, they are far more willing to try and co-operate even in challenging situations.

What keeps us going and how we reboot on bad days

Deborah shared with us an illustration that deeply resonated with her, and which reflects the theme of this chapter. It shows a lioness with her cub, and the lioness has her heard turned in the direction of the cub thinking: *'When I feel like giving up, I turn around and look at who is looking at me'.*

'When I feel like giving up, I turn around and look at who is looking at me.'

We are giving up our time to help others, as we do at home all the time. We also have to re-live times in our lives that we would sometimes rather forget. However, we do not regret giving so much of our time to NVR, because of what we gain from it: life-changing testimonies and the experience of seeing others changing their lives in front of our eyes. This process has made us the people who we are today: confident, strong-willed and positive-minded. Attending the NVR parenting groups reminds us of how far we have come. It has restored our faith in humanity.

We sometimes still cry or get upset when connecting with someone else's story or reading our self-announcements. There are still large parts of our experiences and the people we were that we do not want to go back to, or remember how bad things were. We see this as a form of self-preservation. With the re-telling of our stories, we can go back and reveal a little bit more about ourselves, which allows us a bit more self-forgiveness and self-empathy each time we do. We also still feel embarrassed and ashamed, and sometimes need to revisit our commitment to NVR and the purpose of why we are persisting with it. The changes in others and when seeing the positive sides that were uncovered in the rainbow basket in all their relationships, gives us a huge sense of fulfillment and achievement. We nearly always leave the groups we participate in on a high, particularly at the end of the 12th week. The mindfulness (glossary, p87) at the end of each session is so important, because it allows some stillness and peace of mind that may not be yet available at home.

We bounce off each other as well and trigger new ideas and memories, thus supporting each other's development. Our relationships with each other have deepened, although we do more things together than 'normal friends'. We know about each other more than our friends know about us. Because we have developed a deep trust as a result of working together participating in the NVR work, we know each other in a way that we don't share with our friends outside of NVR but that strengthens us in our individual life journey. Our participation satisfies a sense of passion. NVR has turned everything that we had learned before in society on the head: acts of kindness rather than punishments and rewards.

We now share these beliefs and have become a community that wants to keep growing with these values and beliefs.

For us, it is exciting to meet other people who have heard about NVR and who are curious about it.

We keep going because, at the end of the day, we feel we have made a difference, and that reboots us. We keep our own presence intact, even though we might come across an emotionally challenging situation. When that happens, we show empathy, compassion and care, but do not get drawn into the negative emotions of the moment. That does not mean that we might not express emotions ourselves, because we show empathy, compassion, love and care. This sometimes even makes us tearful, when we connect with our own and others' pain. We also express joyfulness and hug parents, when celebrating their achievements and successes. The strength of a group is that everybody joins in any individual's success and gets excited, and it becomes a collective success that everybody feels part of in the network. When things do not go so well we empathise and reach out with words of encouragement and hope, because nobody wants to leave anyone behind. It is not a race but rather a collective endeavour: if anyone loses or hurts in the group, there has to be a group effort to contain it and bring the person back to a place where they can persist and move forward. We have a sense of collective responsibility within the group.

Absences are noticed and acted upon by the group. For example, Lesley remembered a parent who argued in the group and struggled to come back afterwards. And yet the group sent her a card: 'We are missing you – we want you to come back'. She did come back and revealed a bit more about herself and finished the whole course.

In one of our specialist groups, a grandmother had to bring her baby granddaughter. The whole group supported her with that. It benefitted the group reminding everyone how moving it is to first hold a baby. It also reflected the grandmother's commitment to attend despite difficult circumstances at home, giving her group members a lot of respect for her level of commitment.

Another grandmother turned up with an oxygen tank on wheels that was attached to her nose. These two examples demonstrate the level that people go to in order to attend NVR groups. It humbles us and gives us a lot of respect for human suffering.

We are not trying to give suggestions, recipes and solutions, but introduce the NVR approach and skills, offering the connection to seeing these tools and attitudes applied in real life situations. Our examples and life experiences bring them alive, ignited through the belief of all that it can work to improve peoples' lives and relationships. Every week we learn something new. New parents have so much to offer to everyone. Participating and learning from them prevents us from returning to our own despair.

Another key aspect of relating with each other that takes us 'beyond differences', is to aim for a non-judgemental, trusting and open relationship with each other. Our stories and humanity and our willingness to be open and show our own vulnerability disarms new parents' suspicion and guardedness. Parents pick up that we have open, relaxed and trusting relationships with each other and with the professionals, which makes them feel safe, contained and supported, thereby modelling and mirroring the types of relationships that we promote.

We try to offer ourselves to the group and are not deliberately trying to manipulate them into feeling compelled to submit to what we are saying. On the contrary, we know that it only works effectively if they find their own voice and a way to move through their individual experiences. However, if they are open, trusting and non-defensive, they can listen deeply and select what is relevant to them. These connections go beyond differences of class, gender, race, culture, age and religion, to name just a few of the lenses that John Burnham and others call the GRRAACCEES (Burnham *et al*, 2008). We are also mindful of stories lived and stories told, the untold and unheard stories, the unknown and untellable stories and of the storytelling itself, all described by Barnet Pearce in the acronym LUUUUTT (Pearce, 2007, p212).

This also goes beyond pity, but enables compassion, empathy, endurance, humility and love in the context of shared pain and suffering.

We discussed whether we should have parents from different backgrounds or having mixed gender groups. Although we agreed that it is not essential for the general message of the NVR approach, a variety of voices can give different perspectives and another flavour, and is beneficial for the delivery of the group. It is useful to include fathers' perspectives. As we have already discussed in part 3, in our experience, couples often improve their relationship and work from the same script when attending groups together.

We think that, for men, the presence of other men in the groups helps them to open up more, as beautifully described by Louise's husband, who has now become an active ambassador of the benefits of NVR in the outside world:

> *'I did not think the gender of the participants mattered, when I attended. We were all parents together, trying to do the best for our children. However, on reflection, I was pleased that I was not the only male there. There were a couple of other men participating in the group, and we had one male graduate parent. This male graduate parent was not afraid to share with us the challenges that he faced, including that he had to learn to parent his second child differently from the first. I think if I had been the only man there, I may have felt 'ganged up' on. I may not have been so open'.*

Summary of Part 4

We only know that our participation works thanks to the feedback given by the parents and from the changes that we see happening during the process of the group sessions. New parents often come for a chat once a session has finished and tell us how much they have appreciated our contributions. The participants' appreciation of us keeps us attending in the future, and nothing else could be more rewarding and fulfilling for us. They tell us that us being there keeps them returning every week.

We remind them of a spider building its web, when we explain the concept of persistence in NVR.

Persistence reminds us of spiders building its web: if someone destroys it, they start again from scratch.

The uniqueness and key difference in the delivery of the participatory NVR approach is its constant embodiment[13], enacted through us as participating graduate parents and through a multitude of embodied exercises, roleplays and sculpts that we ask parents to immerse themselves in. We believe that actions speak louder than words, and when we 'perform' and enact together, NVR works and comes alive. Knowledge and practice become one but are experienced differently by everyone. This happens in bite-sized chunks rather than in big jumps. The practice always has many funny sides, including a whole range of emotions that we welcome and encourage. Hard work is more easily done with humour and laughter. We have a deep

13 We are deeply indebted to the work of Augusto Boal and his theatre of the oppressed and to Jakob Moreno's Psychodrama and therapeutic action model, and many exercises that we picked up from Uri Weinblatt, Bruno Koerner and Martin Lemme inspired us when putting the NVR ideas and tools into practice with new parents and professionals.

validation for each other, for the new parents, for the NVR ideas, and for our shared humanity, and that is, for us, the secret to why it works so well and is such a transformative experience for so many.

Part 5: What our parent participation model looks like in practice

Interviews and meeting graduate parents

The pre-group interviews are done for all parents with their referrers in two days, each one lasting 30 minutes. During these interviews, the professional facilitators take the pre-group measures, draw a family genogram, find out about support needs, particularly if child care and transport support is required (which the referrers have to deal with), encourage the attendance of fathers, (ex)partners, grandparents or supporters if any are already identified. They then answer questions, give out a handout with dates, times and location of the sessions. After this part of the meeting, the parents have an opportunity to meet up with graduate parent facilitators on their own, who are waiting for them with refreshments.

Graduate parents have a lot of compassion with these new parents and take the time to listen to their concerns about their children's behaviours. They express that they empathise with their experiences and offer sympathy for the difficult time they are going through in their lives. New parents are often extremely fragile and deeply upset with no ray of hope for a better future. Many of them have reached a point of giving up on their child and believe that nothing will work.

Having been in their shoes, graduate parents understand very well where they are at and can approach them with a non-judgemental attitude.

To make the parents feel at ease, the graduate parents offer them tea, coffee and biscuits, while they sit and listen to them. New parents have many questions in relation to graduate parents' experiences of and with NVR.

Normally, two or three graduate parents are in the room with the new parents, taking turns over the two days. When introducing themselves and sharing their own personal experiences, they quickly break the ice. New parents relate easily to them and understand that the graduate parents know what they are going through and how difficult their lives at home are, with no support. They have often experienced how new parents' faces light up when they realise that graduate parents share their difficult experiences of parenting. When new parents are willing to open up to them about their lives, graduate parents feel really honoured.

Some new parents may only stay a short while others may stay for a few hours. Speaking to the graduate parents is sometimes the first time they have been able to offload all their worries, often getting through a lot of tissues. Graduate parents are all aware how important it is for them to be there for the new parents at this time of high need. No amount of time they can spend with them at this point is a waste, nor is it ever too much. Some new parents find it embarrassing to tell others about their difficulties at home. Others feel that they are the ones to blame. After opening up to the graduate parents about what has been going on, a huge sense of relief is written on their faces.

New parents are also very keen to hear more about where graduate parents are today with their children. They want to know more about the NVR tools and how graduate parents have used them in their homes to improve their children's behaviour. The graduate parents then explain how effective the tools and concepts of NVR are, how they have really improved their lives, that they are in a much happier house now, that they have managed to re-build their relationships with their children and regained their parental presence.

At times, new parents remain sceptical about whether the NVR approach will work for them, or they might say, 'My daughter's behaviour needs to change, not mine'. Graduate parents then explain that they used to have exactly the same attitude, but once allowing NVR into their lives they were able to make changes in their parenting and saw massive improvements as a result. They may need to tell the new parents, 'Your child might never change. So you, as the parent, will have to change, and that is the way forward to improve your relationship with your child'.

At this point new parents often ask: 'Does NVR really work? How long did it take you to notice a change?' An answer to these questions is that, 'NVR is not a magic wand. Your problems will not go away overnight. It takes time and persistence. Sometimes you may take five steps forward and three steps back. But it is important to notice the positive steps you have made rather than focus on the negative ones. You also get days where you may slip back to your old style of parenting. This is totally normal. We are only human. However, it is important that you recognise this and start again the next day.'

When asked how long it took them to notice changes, graduate parents may explain that changes may not always been seen straight away, but by the end of the course some of their child's behaviours had improved massively. However, NVR is not a quick fix. It is ongoing. They did the NVR parent group a while ago, they can explain, and they still practice NVR in their daily lives today to keep their family life stable and loving. 'The good thing about NVR for us,' they might say, 'is that once you have the knowledge and understanding of the NVR tools, you are equipped to resolve any challenging situation in a more effective way'.

During the meeting with the new parents, graduate parents offer them to have a quick look through the NVR testimonies booklet and its illustrations. Some parents have commented: 'Oh my goodness, this is exactly how my walls look!' They can relate easily to the sibling aggression pictures. Reading the testimonies helps them to decide that NVR is worth doing.

Meeting graduate parents after their interviews with the professionals has proven to be really successful. New parents often report that, if they had not met graduate parents and listened to their experiences of NVR, they would not have attended the NVR parent group. They often ask if the graduate parents will be attending the parent group, too, as they now feel connected with them and comfortable in their presence.

For graduate parents, it is very rewarding to know that they have been there for the new parents, offered them their support, shared their experiences with them and have given them hope for a better future – one that includes NVR.

Home visits before the specialist group

The specialist groups have a different format than the generic ones. They last longer overall and have longer group sessions (14 weeks instead of 12 weeks, and lasting two hours instead of 90 minutes). The specialist programme also starts with home visits to prepare each individual family for the group.

Home visits are very beneficial for prospective parents. Some parents are in denial about their child's involvement in criminal activities.

When graduate parents attend the home, they are never alone and always accompanied by other professionals. Apart from the facilitators, a social worker, a family support or youth offending team worker may also come along. None of those attending ever knows what to expect when meeting a family and entering their homes – it can sometimes be a very hostile atmosphere and parents keep their guard up.

When doing home visits, the presence of graduate parents, who have been in similar difficult situations is crucial. They keep an open mind and do not show judgement or criticism, but can empathise with and relate to these families, particularly when sharing any stories about their own children's involvement with criminal activities or about their own houses being raided by police, or about their adolescent son or daughter not coming home for weeks. New families often relate to these stories and see that the graduate parents know exactly how traumatic experiences effect the whole family. Graduate parents often tell them that they are not there to preach or judge, but to offer their support and explain to them how NVR can play a big role in changing the difficult situation that they are experiencing.

However, while parents who are visited at home are usually very keen to hear more about NVR and accept and welcome more support, there are some who feel that they cannot trust anyone, or, in situations of gang involvement, they may fear that taking steps might increase the danger towards their child from gang members. Others may worry that they will get into more trouble with the police.

After a few home visits over several weeks, these families are usually a lot clearer about the principles of NVR and some are very eager to start the NVR specialist parent group. By doing the house visits, a trusting relationship with each of the families can be been built until the point where they feel comfortable enough about opening up in front of other families who are in similar situations.

And then there are the parents who will not even open their front doors to us at all, and will not attend the NVR parent group. This is another situation in which persistence has to be practiced, and social workers and family support workers or other professionals will have to offer further one-to-one support to them in their home and try to refer them again at a later stage. While this is frustrating for us, this has been very effective.

Finally, there are the parents who are oblivious to the behaviours of their children outside of the home, or who are more strong-willed and have kept their parental presence in the home, but who demonstrate the fact that parental presence in the home does not automatically equate to parental presence outside the home. And gangs can be very clever: they are good at covering up clues to an individual member's criminal involvement. If an adolescent therefore behaves well in the home and demonstrates love and consideration to their parents, this may only serve to hide their criminal activities outside the home. Parents often have no clue about this until the police knock at their door. In these situations a graduate parent who has experienced this first hand can look past this disguise and support the new parent to face up to this reality.

Participation during the 12-week generic group programme

We start our description of the 12-week generic group programme with an overview of the themes for the sessions and the five-part structure of each session. We usually try to follow these structures in all our generic NVR parent groups.

The generic groups were developed for application in a CAMHS context and for parents whose children presented with a variety of challenges, such as behavioural problems, anxiety, school refusal, ADHD and ASD, to name just a few. The specialist groups were developed later, when we worked in the community, and these targeted parents whose children were affected by gangs or by Child Sexual Exploitation. The specialist groups are longer, starting with up to four weeks of home visits, and they last for 14 weeks instead of 12. The weekly specialist group sessions also last longer – two hours instead of an hour and a half. Each weekly specialist group session starts with a presentation from an agency that has some involvement with children, who are in gangs or at risk of gangs or who are sexually exploited. The generic group starts with what we later in this chapter describe as part 2: the whole group coming together for a welcome and brief presentation of the NVR key principle of the day.

Overview of the 12-week generic group programme

Session 1	De-escalation
Session 2	Parental Presence
Session 3	Baskets
Session 4	Supporters
Session 5	Reconciliation Gestures
Session 6	Active Resistance and Helping Siblings
Session 7	Parents' Trauma and Self Announcement
Session 8	Child's Trauma
Session 9	The Announcement
Session 10	The Sit-in
Session 11	Looking after Yourself
Session 12	Review (Post NVR Outcome Measures)

Five-part structure of each session

In order for the parent group sessions to run efficiently, each session follows a five-part structure to help new trainee and experienced facilitators to work together more productively. This five-part structure is not etched in stone but stands as a basis for facilitators to aid the delivery of the sessions.

Part 1: Pre-session for professional facilitators and graduate parent facilitators (30-45 mins).

Part 2: Whole group work. Welcome, brief review of last week's topic and how parents got on with it at home, presentation of the day's key NVR principle (see above), graduate parent facilitators add their testimonies in relation to key principle of the day (30 min).

Part 3: Small group work, where the key principle is applied to the parents' home situation, exercises, therapeutic work with the participants (45 mins).

Part 4: Whole group work. Brief feedback from the groups, mindfulness exercise (15 mins).

Part 5: Post-Session Review. Graduate parent facilitators and professional facilitators only, review of the small group work, the presentation, attendance, whether some parents need to be followed-up, concerns that may need to be related back to referrers or others (social workers), tasks and themes for next session, text message to be sent in-between sessions (30-45 mins).

Supervision for the generic and specialist groups

Professionals and graduate parent facilitators of both types of groups are required to attend four one-and-a-half-hour supervision meetings by a qualified NVR supervisor during the programme. During the supervision, graduate parents become familiar with reflective systemic practice, often sharing their own questions and observations and contributing to the supervision process, thus offering their specific perspectives and enormously enriching it.

Parent participation in the pre-group session (part 1)

The first part is called the pre-group session, where the graduate parent/s contribute suggestions to the preparation of the session. This is a weekly meeting before the group that lasts for 30 to 45 minutes, to review the schedule for the session and should include confirming which facilitator will take the lead throughout its different aspects. With specialist groups, time has to be incorporated for a guest speaker to link their area of expertise to the NVR principle for that week.

When there is so much to cover but not a lot of time to do it, timekeeping is an important factor. If a facilitator who has taken responsibility for leading in an area of the session is absent, adjustments will need to be made to accommodate this change. Once all the pre-group meeting arrangements are agreed, the room is prepared by arranging the chairs in a circle and setting out the refreshments. The graduate parent/s may also go and greet the parents and tick the attendance in the register.

Parent participation at the beginning of the session (part 2)

Once the new parents come in, they are invited to help themselves to refreshments and a seat. The second part of the session then begins. After a few weeks, the new parents usually start chatting to one another as well as to the facilitators and graduate parents. After the key NVR Principle for that day is introduced by one of the professional facilitators, the graduate parent/s often share their testimony in relation to that principle. Graduate parent facilitators have to adapt the length of their testimony to the presentation and to the time that is available, which is a key skill that requires attention, constructive feedback and experience.

Everyone who presents, including the professional facilitators, should therefore try to be concise and keep to the topic. It is therefore important to be punctual and start on time. Space should also be allowed for the new parents to ask questions. If there is a whole group exercise for that day, it is demonstrated in this part of the session, for example the hand exercises that embodies escalation and de-escalation. This exercise is often demonstrated by two graduate parent facilitators, before the new parents try it for themselves. Embodied exercises like this are an excellent and often preferred way of helping new parents grasp the understanding of the NVR principles that are shared.

Parent participation during the work in small groups (part 3)

During the small group work, parent facilitators may support professional facilitators to work with a parent who may have missed the previous session or with someone who got very upset when reporting about their last week's experience at home. Parent facilitators can be instrumental in showing compassion and empathy to a parent, who may feel lost because they are behind the rest of their small group or express an anxiety over a situation that happened at home. They listen carefully but do not judge the parent, who just needs support.

On one occasion, one member of a small group was very distraught because she felt that she might not be able to continue coming, as she had to support her daughter by taking care of her granddaughter. The group agreed for her to bring her granddaughter to the sessions and, when that happened, group members and facilitators took turns helping her to hold the baby. She was so grateful and managed to continue the whole course.

Parent participation at the end of the session (part 4)

Usually, each session ends with a mindfulness exercise, which for some parents is the only opportunity to have a calm moment to themselves and reflect on thoughts that are peaceful, often allowing them the strength to deal with the challenges they may have to go back home to. Graduate parent facilitators are frequently asked to lead in this area and read from the mindfulness chapter of the handbook. It usually helps new parents to accept the concept of mindfulness when they experience it delivered by a graduate parent facilitator, even when it had appeared strange to them at first. Reading the mindfulness exercises is a huge skill in itself that graduate parent facilitators acquire gradually and with constructive feedback from everyone involved.

Parent participation during the post-group session (part 5)

The post-group session completes the five-part structure of the group sessions. Clearing up and rearranging chairs is done quickly to allow for the facilitators and graduate parent facilitators to share their observations and ideas about the group and reflect together how the session as a whole went. It allows them to acknowledge whether there were any disclosures or learning points, and whether any improvements could be made.

On one occasion, graduate parents shared a story about one new parent in the post session. This parent had told her small group that she felt that her mother was always very strong and never cried. As a result, she herself now struggled to hide from her own daughter any signs weakness and never allowed herself to cry. However, after starting the NVR group, she had a lengthy conversation with her mum in which she asked her how she managed to never cry and stay so strong. She shared with her small group how deeply shocked she was to hear her mum tell her that she cried in the comfort of her room and then, once she finished, would dry her eyes, come out of her room and face the next challenge. She was surprised and at the same time relieved about her mother's revelations, and became able to release her own frustrations through crying. She then noticed an improvement in her relationship with her own daughter, which was wonderful to hear because her daughter had been taken away from her into care. Everyone in the group was moved by this experience.

During the week that follows the session, a text message is sent to each of the parents to remind them of the next group session, and includes words of encouragement and motivation. New parents have often reported that these texts served them as a reminder to keep pressing forward and not give up.

Participation after the parent group sessions

Parent clubs

During the group sessions, new parents are made aware of the options that graduate parents have after completing the programme. They can either become more involved as volunteer parent facilitators and/or attend the NVR parent club. The parent club initially started after the third parent group programme, and at these parents meet once a month for an hour and half. Sometimes a professional facilitator is present, but mostly not. If there is a need for professional input, the lead parent facilitator may contact them. The location is usually within the service, where the group sessions are normally held. Parents come from different groups. The clubs are parent-lead. Themes have included things like how to maintain the NVR ideas and skills, how to support each other during and after meeting up in the clubs, and how to access professional help if needed.

Parent clubs offer ongoing support for parents once the 12-week sessions have come to an end. There are two different clubs during the month, one held in the morning, the other one in the early evening. This is to enable as many parents as possible access to support. Parents are welcome at both clubs and, if they choose to attend both, they have bi-monthly support.

The atmosphere is relaxed and friendly. Refreshments and a listening ear are always provided. Many of the attending parents become friends for life, which is important, because some have lost contact with their own friends due to their challenging family circumstances.

Usually, club meetings start with everyone saying how things are for them. Those who are in the greatest need speak first. Some ground rules exist: that everyone is respectful, non-judgemental and considerate of each other. All parents are listened to and asked what support they require. Sometimes parents ask to be reminded of one or two of the NVR key principles or skills, or they may say what NVR interventions they applied and ask for feedback and how they could have done them more successfully. At other times they may have forgotten to use the NVR ideas altogether. When this happens, they are reminded that we are all human and that it is always hard to think in the heat of the moment, but are reminded to be persistent. People are never prescribed what they should do, but instead questions are asked in order to help them to find their own solutions. It might be explored with them, for example, whether they tried using one of the NVR key principles that might have helped in the situation. In some cases, it is important to just be there with a tissue and a sympathetic ear.

Different types of people come along to the clubs. There is a core group of people who have been practising NVR for a long time and who attend every parent club. Their children have now grown up, left home and are living lives of their own, but they still return month after month to support other parents who are experiencing life as a struggle. Then there are a few new parents, who have just completed the 12-week sessions. Finally, there are those who attend whenever they feel they are in need. Anyone who can attend is welcome.

There have been some very difficult situations in which attendees had been in desperate need. NVR can be a long journey: just when you think that things can't get any worse, you find out that it can. In those circumstances, the other graduate parents usually recommend that the person continues to practise NVR. They also suggest professional places or people who they can contact for further help. The clubs are self-help support groups of volunteers, and sometimes people need more than support and a listening ear from their peers, but professional help.

Through working with the NVR parent groups, all graduate parents have become knowledgeable about what type of professional help is available in the local community. Over time, they also got to know some professionals who work in diverse local services and who can advise further on how parents who attended an NVR group in the past can be referred. During or after the parent club, there is also telephone or e-mail access to a professional NVR facilitator, who can offer advice when needed.

But it is not all doom and gloom. Parents love to celebrate achievements, both big and small, such as a parent's success story in using NVR during difficult times and succeeding with their child. Parents are genuinely happy to hear when someone in the club or their young person at home has accomplished something, whatever that might mean for that particular child or parent and however small it might be. They all rejoice together.

Even when leaving the parent club, parents often keep a life-line going with phone calls, text messages or cards. Although this may sound like a bit of a cliché, graduate parents often compare themselves to a big family. They cry together, laugh together and celebrate together.

Newsletters

Graduate parents have had some great opportunities to participate in publicity. They have voiced their opinions in the 27 newsletters that have been produced covering all topics of NVR, including the shame-conference and sit-in masterclass with Uri Weinblatt in 2014 or a trip abroad to participate in the international NVR conference in Munich, Germany, where the four attending parents were called the Four Mothers by Haim Omer. In one of the newsletters, a parent author of this book presented her e-mail correspondence with Uri Weinblatt, where she gave him feedback on shame, sharing with him how listening to his take was an eye-opener and a steep learning curve for her. Before the conference she had not even been aware of how her own behaviour as parent had caused shame to her son.

Uri's concept of 'recovering conversations' was of great help to the graduate parents, too. It gave them an alternative way to do sit-ins with their children. Uri had demonstrated that a recovering conversation can be considered as success when parents and children are having a two-way conversation in a calm way.

Uri shared in his master class that in a recovering conversation with two parents it is more effective if a parent who has lost their parental presence uses 'I' instead of 'we', in order to avoid blaming the child or putting shame on them. Graduate parents found this idea difficult to accept as they had always told new parents to stay united and work together during the sit-in, using 'we' so that the young person knows that her parents are both working together, particularly if they had previously been divided in their approach. After sharing this confusion, Uri explained his own approach in more detail, at the same time reassuring the graduate parents that he fully understood their views as well.

He explained in his response that if the weaker parent who has lost their parental presence in the home uses the word 'I' , this will help them get their parental presence back. Their child will see that this 'weaker parent' is equal to the strong parent, who has not lost their parental presence. The child will still see them as equals working together.

It was really nice for the graduate parents that Uri took the time to respond to their questions, concerns and suggestions in detail and agreed that this correspondence could be published in our newsletter so that all had a clearer understanding and were able to use these new ideas in the future.

The newsletters were also used to announce important upcoming dates in the local NVR networks, such as the monthly parent club dates or sibling picnic days.

Editing and writing the parent testimonies booklet

Apart from writing in newsletters, graduate parents have also edited and written in the second parent booklet about many aspects of their and their family's lived experiences, such as sibling rivalry or the impact of the children's challenging behaviours on their other children and on others. They have raised awareness of how easy it is for adolescents to be groomed into gangs and sexual exploitation. Like the monthly newsletters, the parent testimony booklet aimed to help parents gain knowledge about these problems and give them more choices and ways to respond. The testimonies booklet was kept in the same format as its predecessor, the green parent booklet, so that parents and others can use them in conjunction. When graduate parents got together to co-write the book of testimonies, they were excited to be part of this project. They felt passionate about how effective NVR is and wanted all the voices of graduate NVR parents to be heard by other parents. It was not an easy task to put the booklet together, as there were so many testimonies to choose from.

After weeks of shuffling bits of paper, they decided to write chapters in the booklet about supporters, fathers, siblings and mothers. The illustrations were drawn by Rosie-May[14], the younger daughter of one of the contributing parents, who had difficulty talking at the time. She could only express through her pictures how difficult life at home was. The graduate parents did not want the testimonies booklet to be in black-and-white and they therefore chose a different colour border around each chapter.

Afterwards, they felt very proud of this book. Every parent, child and supporter can relate to the multiple testimonies that had been written, whether by a parent, a supporter, a father, a sibling or even by the children with challenging behaviour themselves. The book is now used for many purposes: training days, NVR parent groups, individual work with parents, etc. and still holds the power to inspire others to do NVR. The process of editing and discussion, as well as choosing the testimonies and illustrations, gave them great confidence in writing and publicising and prepared them well for further tasks in the world of media and publicity, like this current publication.

Interviewing Haim Omer during the filming of a DVD about the first International NVR Conference in London

When some graduate parents were asked if they would like to take part in a film during and after the first international NVR conference in London in 2011, to promote their experiences of NVR and help encourage other parents to attend the NVR parent group, they felt this was a great opportunity. Their confidence had increased noticeably since doing NVR, and they wanted to share this with all those parents who were still going through the difficulties they had.

During the conference, they had the opportunity to meet Haim Omer in person and interview him. It felt to them like meeting with God himself.

14 It is also Rosie-May who has done the wonderful illustrations for this book.

Haim had not only invented NVR, he was their life saviour and they all thought that he deserved a medal.

They were very excited and overwhelmed by the experience of meeting him and very nervous, too, about choosing the questions that they wanted to ask him. They all had many, and decided to ask two questions each, such as: *'How did you come up with NVR? Have you ever had to use NVR in your own personal life?'* Haim told them that he used NVR with his sons. They then asked whether NVR works for every child, even a child with autistic traits. He told them that he believes that it does work with every child. Another question was about starting a monthly NVR parent club, to offer more support after the NVR parent group. They asked him, whether he could give them any ideas about how to get it up and running. He advised persistence, to start small, advertise it well and put the word out to the parents by writing testimonies. They followed his advice and it worked: the parent club is now continuously growing.

They were amazed about how easily Haim Omer was lip-reading all their questions. They would have never noticed that he was nearly deaf. They were very pleased to have had the opportunity of meeting him, of talking to him and getting to know him as the down-to-earth man he is. He managed to put their nerves completely at rest, as if they had known him for ages.

Interviewing each other for the DVD

At times, graduate parents are asked by professionals to take part in filming to promote NVR to other parents, so that they have a clearer understanding of the principles of NVR. Filming can also be done for professional training, so that professionals understand how NVR has improved our lives by watching testimonies and interviews, rather than learning about the NVR principles reading a book. We have also been involved in filming during a conference to promote NVR to others.

When taking part in filming, it is important that we look back over the footage, before the final picture is shown to others. At times, we noticed mistakes that needed to be adjusted. On some occasions, the filming had not been up to standard, due to poor lighting, and had to be repeated. In other instances we had to edit the film to protect our confidentiality and had to take out our real names or had to shorten the piece.

Graduate parents could be asked to be filmed while doing a role play when taking part in a specific NVR exercise, for example participating in a sit-in. Some graduate parents were not happy with the filming until it finally became perfect and fitted their expectations. Equally, we also edited anything that we had co-written before it was published until we became happy with the final texts. This way we learned that any piece of text, film or testimony can be re-visited many times, until it eventually fits the purpose and the audience for which it was produced. Graduate parents also interviewed each other for the DVD that was produced during the first international NVR conference in 2011, developing their own questions, taking turns as interviewers and interviewees. They asked questions like:

- Where else can you see NVR working?
- What benefits has NVR made to yourself as a parent?
- Do you think NVR was worthwhile doing?
- What can you see happening in the future'?
- How was your life before NVR?
- Which one has been the most effective NVR tool for you?
- When did you first notice changes in your family life?
- How did your child react when you were using the NVR tools?
- How are you as a family now?
- If you could encourage another parent to do NVR, what would you say to them?

They spoke honestly and were very pleased with the outcome of these interviews. The interviews from this DVD are often now shown to new parents before they take part in the NVR parent group, or to professionals in training.

Mentoring and support for new graduate parent facilitators

A more recent development is the training of experienced parent facilitators to become mentors for new parent facilitators, who are starting to support groups. Mentoring training was developed to introduce them to the various concepts and skills that they would need to mentor others. All three graduate parents of this book attended the 12-week mentoring course. Alongside the training, mentor trainees had to practise what they had learned with a new graduate parent, who wanted to become a parent facilitator. They were closely supervised and reported back weekly to their mentoring course facilitators and their peers. Every three weeks, they were observed by their trainers while they were mentoring. Alongside the mentoring training, the mentees were co-facilitating a parent group for the first time. Their group facilitators were aware of the mentoring that they were undertaking and had to report on the improvements that they were making, when giving their testimonies or reading the mindfulness exercises in the groups. The mentees also gave weekly feedback on their mentoring sessions, as well as a final feedback. This created a full 360-degree feedback cycle, which proved to be highly effective.

During the mentoring course, mentor trainees learned about many concepts of mentoring. Among others, they covered listening skills in detail: the difference between listening and hearing, active listening and the barriers to listening, and being able to listen without judging, which is an essential part of mentoring another person. This is especially important when someone is revealing aspects of themselves that completely go against their mentor's own values. They learnt about empathy, non-verbal communication, the power of silence, questioning skills and non-violent communication (NVC).

Once they had the basic skills, they needed to find a mentee. This proved to be more difficult for some than others. All of them were juggling a difficult family life with their commitments to volunteer. Agreeing to commit to being involved in the mentoring project meant that people were not only helping to facilitate the parent groups for four hours a week but also attended an hour of mentoring on top each week. This is a huge commitment, and there were also issues with travelling to and from a mutually convenient venue. For these reasons, a few potential mentees felt that they could not take advantage of the mentoring on offer. This was a huge disappointment for those needing a mentee to complete the training. Eventually, however, they all found a mentee who was prepared to commit themselves.

The first task was to write an agreement/contract, covering areas such as how often they would meet, the length of each sessions time keeping, methods of contact should they not be able to meet etc. Then they needed to set goals. This involved exploring their values and why they were volunteering. Most of the goals were around confidence, self-esteem, learning more about specific NVR principles and how to tell their individual stories in a concise and appropriate way. The goals had to be SMART:

S = specific
M = measurable
A = attainable
R = realistic/relevant
T = time-bound.

The mentors were also taught to use the GROW model as a basis for the actual mentoring sessions. This acronym stood for **g**oal-setting, **r**eflection and review, **o**ptions and the **w**-questions: when, where and what.

To be able to do this, they needed to become experts at asking open questions. During the training, mentor trainees were, for example, in one of their training sessions each asked to choose privately a box from a selection placed on a table. Afterwards they had to ask each other open questions to see if the questioner could identify the chosen box. This was a fun activity that helped them to learn about open questions and what types of questions were most effective. They also learned about body language and about how facial expressions can show how people are feeling. This knowledge enabled them to adjust their line of questioning. Mentoring is not about giving advice or finding solutions, but about helping someone to find their own path to overcoming their issues.

In the same way that graduate parent facilitators are usually surprised by the openness of new parents when they first meet them, the mentor trainees were astonished by the personal revelations that their mentees made to them. They discovered that a mentee's goals could change over several sessions. One mentee, for example, realised that not only did she need to improve her ability to tell her story in a concise and relevant manner, she also needed to improve her own self-respect and learn how to say 'no'. This became quite a dominant aspect of her mentoring, and her mentor had to be careful to keep the mentoring sessions relevant to NVR mentoring, as it could have quite easily become a counselling session. Therefore, this mentor trainee was extremely reliant on the trainer to help her work that difference through. She e-mailed her after every meeting and received guidance about what had been done during the meeting while also developing a plan for the following session.

The mentor trainees used several techniques to help their mentees to achieve their goals, depending on what was required at the time. They role-played, for example, when one of the mentees wanted to know more about the different types of sit-in. The mentor could take the place of both the parent and the child, to allow the mentee to feel what it is like to be in both positions. They found this highly enlightening.

They learned a great deal from their mentoring experience. One mentee shared in her observed mentoring meeting that she had left a note on the bathroom mirror telling her 11-year old son how pleased she was that he had hung up his wet towel after having a bath. Her intention was to publicly praise him and make him feel good. However, her son got angry and told her that he felt ashamed as a result of that note because it was something he should be doing anyway. This is a great example of how praise can bring about shame, despite good intentions. The mentee was encouraged to make this story part of her testimony in relation to shame.

Regardless of their ups and downs during the training and mentoring, all mentor trainees were successful. One professional facilitator fed back at the end of the course: 'During the mentoring process [name of mentee] has progressed from unconscious incompetence through to conscious competence after her individual NVR mentoring sessions.'

All mentees also reported back that they had reached their goals. All three mentor trainees qualified. This mentoring programme will soon be written into all Level 2 and 3 group facilitator training packages in order to enable good training and peer support for new graduate parents who want to become parent facilitators. This way, a network and pool of highly qualified and passionate graduate parents can be created and retained, who are able and willing to join and support any new parent group at short notice. If the pool is big enough, there is no danger of overstretching individual graduate parents or overusing them.

Participation during professional training for facilitators and others

One of the three parent authors, Deborah, started her NVR journey as a parent looking for hope, but remained resistant to attend a 12-week specialist group programme, which she eventually only agreed to in order to get social services off her back. She began the specialist NVR group in October 2014. When she finished the programme she was pleasantly surprised and honoured to be invited to help with a new group that was starting in 2015. She had to register as a volunteer with Oxleas NHS Foundation Mental Health Trust to get her travel costs covered and to be formally accepted as a volunteer. Little did she know that this was the beginning of a new chapter in her life.

Deborah found the move from being a parent during the 12-week parent group to becoming a graduate parent facilitator intense at times, because of the emotional demands that could sometimes be made on her, and for which she was completely unprepared. She realised that, no matter how organised everyone might have been before, there was no way to ever truly know what might trigger an emotional response from a parent. Parents generally listened and soaked up every word like sponges, hoping to find solutions to their challenges at home, but there were times when some parents did not agree or just could not understand the principles. At these points, Deborah would give details of her own lived experience, which they later reported helped them comprehend what was previously presented. It gave her a very uplifting feeling to hear this feedback, and to know that her own hardship had helped them to understand NVR better.

After participating in another specialist group as a graduate parent facilitator, she completed a four-day level 1 certificate, training together with a group of professionals who she had once felt frustrated with, but she now understood the restrictions and limitations of their jobs within which they had to work. This Level 1 training covered all the principles in NVR at an introductory level, which included the history of NVR, embodied exercises and small group work, where the principles were applied to ongoing cases that the professionals had been asked to share.

Having this experience really helped her to emphasise when, over the next few years, she attended further Level 1 training courses as a graduate parent together with the professional trainers. Each group of professionals on that level were different and brought a variety of personalities and questions that sometimes challenged the trainers and her. For example, she was often asked whether she really believed that NVR genuinely worked. She would tell the professionals who had asked this question that having the ability to use NVR was like having a driver's license which always still leaves the choice whether to drive, walk, ride a bicycle or take a bus.

She shared her testimony at different stages during the training and also answered individual questions from the attendees. Most if not all of the professionals who attended the Level 1 training left wanting to utilise the NVR principles that they had learned within their professional contexts.

After supporting several parent groups and Level 1 training for professionals, the parent-author of this book then had the opportunity to complete the eight-day Level 2/3 training over eight months. She was initially worried about the amount of work and commitment involved, but decided that she had nothing to lose and everything to gain. Each training session gave her more in-depth information about the NVR principles, as well as teaching her the necessary skills to become a more experienced parent facilitator. She did a poster presentation, like the other professional trainees, and completed a clinical journal and a 2000-word reflective essay. There were times when she questioned herself, asking herself why she was putting herself through these extra challenges, but she decided that it was good to push herself and to be an example to her children of how working hard helps to achieve goals. It worked: her children were impressed with her hard work, especially with the essay writing. After eight long months, she received her Level 2/3 certificate during a graduation ceremony. One of her daughters had just finished her first year at university and they both took a much-deserved short break in Malta as a way to celebrate their achievements.

When she was later asked to help co-facilitate a new Level 2/3 training for professionals, she knew from her own experience, what the trainees had to face: not only did they have to attend the eight training days but also had to run a 12-week parent group alongside the training. She was grateful that she had remained on the Level 2/3 training and she helped a new group of professional trainees to co-facilitate a parent group, which meant leaving her comfort zone and travelling to a different area from where she lived. The tool book for parents contained all the important information about the course topics that had to be covered. She offered the new trainees valuable tips such as keeping a notebook with the clinical hours and dates for the reflective journal. She understood well when they felt frustrated and did not believe that they could finish the course. Some of the trainees had to overcome personal traumas, but nevertheless persisted until the end and received their certificates. During the graduation ceremony with invited special guest speakers, she was asked to sing with her two daughters (one of whom she originally came to NVR for) a special song that is always played at similar NVR celebrations: *'Something inside so strong'*, by Labi Siffre.

Because of a shortage of trainees, she also acted as a third facilitator for one of the parent groups. Often there was a crisis happening on the day which shortened the preparation sessions. They also had to run the small groups in the same room, which already felt overcrowded during the whole group. The debrief time was also often reduced, due to one of the facilitators having to help run another parent group shortly after the first group. They managed to make it work, however, by being extremely organised and respectful of one another. In this professional context, a lot of data had to be collected for various departments. Each week, a lead trainee facilitator would be agreed. This parent group had a few drops-outs due to ill health, as well as translation and transportation issues. However, some parent graduates from this group were sharing their experiences in the presence of graduate parents from the other groups, professionals, referrers and service managers during the graduation ceremony for parents and trainee facilitators.

She did not realise that what had started as an exercise in resistance as a devastated parent without much hope would lead to years of her helping to train other parents and professionals. She never imagined that her painful experience as a parent would lead her to paid work as a graduate parent facilitator in several Level 1 and Level 2/3 training courses. Later on she also completed the mentoring training course. All this helped her to not only reconnect a badly-disconnected relationship with her own daughter but to touch so many other lives and help them reconnect with their child/children and become graduate parents in NVR.

Participation in presentations, national and international conferences

In 2015, three graduate parents, including two of the parent authors of this book, accompanied Elisabeth to a conference in Witten Herdecke, Germany. Although the three had met each other before, they were not well acquainted. They met several times before the conference to prepare a short presentation based on their NVR journeys. During this time, they got to know each other well. They had all been involved in NVR programmes in different ways. One of them had specialised in the gangs' project, another had a special interest in child exploitation and the third had a child with a diagnosis of high-functioning autism. Whoever would believe that they had anything in common? They all came from varied backgrounds and their family make-up could not have been more different. However, while working together to create a presentation on their individual journeys, they formed a bond that became stronger than many friendships.

One thing that connected them was that they had all grown in confidence. Before attending the NVR groups, they had all felt helpless and thought that they had tried everything. They believed that they had failed as parents and could not see where life was going for their families, or even if their families could survive. Yet at the point where they were to present at the conference in Germany, they were confident that each of their families would survive and even thrive, even though they still had their occasional ups and downs.

They arrived in Düsseldorf, took a taxi to the hotel in Witten-Herdecke, and had a typical German meal that was far better than any German food in England. They met Haim Omer at breakfast along with a few other people who were all attending the conference and who were incredibly pleased to meet them when they learned that they were parents giving a talk at the conference.

They had the opportunity to listen to the other speakers, one of whom was Uri Weinblatt. They were introduced to the audience in the morning and became surprised and overwhelmed during the lunch break by all the people who wanted to talk to them. That afternoon they presented their journeys from hopelessness to confidence.

At some point during the conference they had told Uri Weinblatt about their plans to return to the hotel by bus, on their own, and were surprised when he, too, was at the bus stop. All of them had attended a two-day workshop that Uri had run the previous year, in 2014, when they had met him first and he had become a bit of a hero to them all since then. When they asked him at the bus stop where he was going, he told them that it depended where they were getting off because he did not want them to get lost in a strange country. That was when they realised that, not only was he clever and insightful, but he was also very kind and generous, too. They spent that evening with people who were all attending the conference and together they had a fantastic time.

After returning home, they continued to work together on several projects, and their bond has grown ever since, even though one of the three is now working full time.

The specialist group was the basis for preparing a presentation during the NVR International Conference in Malmo, Sweden, in 2016. Four graduate parent facilitators, including Deborah Frimpong, and three professional facilitators, did this presentation together.

They shared the complexities and horrors that the parents of the specialist parent group and their young people were exposed to and experiencing. With their permission, the presentation in Sweden included some of these stories. Deborah used her poster from her recently completed Level 2/3 course during the presentations in Sweden as part of the visual illustrations. Another graduate parent had had to get her first passport because she had never travelled abroad before. She was initially very nervous but by the time they all came back from Sweden she had developed into a much more confident person, who now still helps run NVR groups for the local NHS Trust. Haim Omer congratulated them after the presentation, telling them that he was very impressed with their work and that he had been in tears during their presentation.

It was not all work, however. They met many international professionals from different parts of the world and even managed to go on a sightseeing tour and a boat trip. Once again, NVR helped open the door for them to not only share their stories and help others, but also to expand their life experience by travelling to parts of the world they had never been to before. They worked hard to produce a successful presentation and will always be remembered as the graduate parents that had presented about their involvement in NVR among their professional peers.

Summary of part 5

We hope that readers can see, from the many examples in what you have just read, how varied parent participation has become and how it has extended the experience and confidence of the parents involved, while at the same time stretching the ability of those professionals who have included them in their work, their contexts and in their professional perspective. Graduate parents have become ambassadors of NVR, taking their testimonies and lived experiences beyond the borders of their borough, their town and their country, encouraging others with their messages of hope and with their confidence that NVR can work for them as well, and that the connection and relationship with children, young people and each other is paramount and more important than correcting behaviours.

Parent participation requires ongoing nurturing and appreciation. Graduate parents still experience ups and down, sometimes needing reminders, support and encouragement that they can pick up threads from before and move forward. However, their peer networks and bonds have grown very strong and have gone beyond the bonds that many friendships or family relationships can provide them with.

Conclusion

We hope this book has demonstrated, with lived examples, how and why parent participation in NVR has worked for us and for others.

We weaved together Paulo Freire's liberation concepts with narrative ideas from Michael White and David Epston and from the Just Therapy members, and systemic principles and practices, and produced our own notions of participation, applying them to NVR parent groups and the training of professional facilitators. The three parents described how they and their individual families managed to overcome hopelessness and helplessness, and how they developed self-efficiency using the ideas of NVR as guidelines. We discussed the commonalities and differences between their stories and highlighted what was significant in liberating them from the grip of their troubles and helping them and their children to reconnect again, and to develop long-lasting respectful and loving relationships. All three committed themselves to the wider NVR community, made their testimonies available to support new parents and professionals, and thus participated in co-creating and embodying the effectiveness of the NVR approach and bringing it alive.

We showed that the goal of our work in NVR is not to help a single person, either the parent or the child, but it is about healing the relationship and the connection between them both, helping a parent to move from a position of 'You' (the child) are wrong via 'I (the parent) am wrong' to 'We (you and I) and our supportive network and wider community are in this together and respect and love each other'.

We have shared in this book our learning that this process often happens in bite size chunks rather than in big jumps; that it is unpredictable and cannot be planned or copied. But we have faith in the following ingredients: a deep validation for ourselves and others; a readiness to open ourselves to our own vulnerability and share our stories of pain and hurt with others; and allowing others to support and contain us in our process of forgiveness. This can include offering forgiveness to ourselves and to others as well as asking for their forgiveness, and then letting healing and re-connection take its natural course.

We hope we have made these transformative ideas and experiences accessible and transparent to a wider audience, and to have encouraged readers to follow the advice of one of our parents in her short message to new parents: 'Just give it a go!'

Glossary of NVR terms

Key concepts in Non-violent Resistance

Classic NVR ideas

Parental presence: A child's or young person's sense that their parent is there for them, that the parent is a safe, solid and dependable person who can be relied upon. A child's sense that their parent knows their whereabouts and cares what they are doing. The child knows what their parent's values are and what they believe regarding right and wrong.

Loss of Parental Presence: Parents are supported to acknowledge fluctuations in their levels of involvement and the presence they have in their child's physical, emotional and social lives, and how they relate to the development of unacceptable behaviours. By exploring their own experiences, unmet needs and developing an inter- and intra-personal awareness, parents affirm their parental values and become conscious of how they communicate them. This helps them to (re-)build their parental presence.

Rebuilding the relationship: When relationships have become characterised by challenging, harmful and self-destructive behaviours there are very few opportunities for people to relate more positively. The relationship needs to be rebuilt based on acknowledging the negative, escalatory patterns within it and committing to learning to adopt new, connecting patterns of behaviour.

De-escalation: Parents learn to identify when things are escalating and to step out of the situation. Two types of escalation tend to occur: one where both sides escalate, and the escalation may end in violence, and another where the parent chooses to give in. Parents often do both. In NVR, parents learn to wait until things are calm and *respond* instead of *react*. This is referred to by the maxim '*strike when the iron is cold*'.

Breaking the silence: Parents tell others about the child's difficult behaviour, how they feel hopeless and helpless about it, and that they need help.

Supporters: Parents identify individuals who can support them and their child. They are specific about how they want these people to help them resist the young person's challenging behaviours.

Reconciliation gestures (or 'relational gestures'): Parents may make regular, small gestures of unconditional love and kindness towards their child. These may be small gifts (items of food, repairs to things that have been broken, special messages, watching the child's favourite TV programme) that are given irrespective of how the child has behaved and without expecting anything in return nor pointing out the act of kindness to the child. Reconciliation gestures are intended to help the parent enact feelings of warmth and love. If the gesture is spurned, parents do not react.

Active resistance: Parents choose to resist attempts to engage them in escalation. They resist the temptation to have the last word. Parents engage in peaceful protest against harmful behaviour. Parents stop giving in to unreasonable demands (internet access throughout the night, bribing the child to attend school, unlimited taxi and laundry services).

Announcement: Parents carefully construct an announcement they will make to their child explaining that they are going to resist their negative behaviour, that they love their child and they want things to be better. They commit to a non-violent stance (verbal and physical). There are no threats or warnings. The announcement is short and specific. Parents practise making the announcement until it embodies and resonates with both their love for their child and their stance of resistance.

Sit-in: If the child repeats the behaviour/s that were addressed in the NVR announcement (for example, punching a sibling), parents will plan a sit-in. They will enter the child's bedroom and sit down and tell them in a calm and quiet way, that they are there to assist the child in thinking of ways forward and to change things. They offer to assist the child in thinking about ways forward. Then they sit quietly or silently for a period of time, to demonstrate their love and their commitment to working towards change in a peaceful way.

Helping siblings and others: By taking time to listen to their experiences and explaining the changes in approach, parents support siblings and others who have been impacted by the child's destructive behaviours.

Tailing and telephone round: When young people run away from home, truant from school, or stay out at night rather than returning home at an appointed time, the risk of harm befalling them increases. Some of these risks include drug misuse, gang involvement, child sexual exploitation and rape, drug dealing and trafficking. The physical and psychological harm to the young person tends to be significant, and parents or other caregivers lose parental presence when the young person withdraws from their sphere of influence. 'Tailing' reverses this process. By 'leaving footprints in dangerous places', caregivers strategically raise their presence with people and in places the young person frequents, e.g. by meeting the parents of other vulnerable young people the child has contact with, gathering contact details, communicating with other adults and young people when their child has not come home, and seeking to find the young person's whereabouts. In the telephone round, caregivers contact a wide range of people who may be able to communicate with their child. It is important to persist in these efforts, time and again, when young people show a pattern of absconding.

Campaign of Concern: Originally called 'message campaign' by Haim Omer, concern is the attitude or mindset in which we would like the family to communicate with the young person after a problematic or positive incident. The support network is informed by parents or other caregivers of such an incident, and the parents nominate certain supporters to approach their child by text, email, letter, video call or in person. In case of a problematic incident (a 'small basket behaviour' – see Three Baskets, below), each supporter expresses their concern for everyone affected by the incident, including the young person who has instigated it. The messages should be neither blaming nor minimising. There should be at least as many 'positive incident' messages as 'problematic incident' messages. Positive incidents are exceptions to the problem – e.g. when the young person has controlled themselves during an argument rather than resorting to aggression as in the past – or an example that shows the young person beginning to thrive or reconnect with other family members, e.g. when they have become able to sit through a maths lesson which they had previously been unable to, or when they have had a meal with their parents, as they used to in the past. In the campaign of concern, the support network becomes a containing social environment for the child or young person.

Innovative developments in NVR

Three Baskets (Uri Weinblatt, adapted from Ross Greene): Parents prioritise unwanted behaviours by placing them in three differently sized imaginary baskets. The large basket contains the largest number of behaviours, that can be let go of for now. The medium-sized basket is for behaviours to compromise over and the small basket is for the one or two most serious and dangerous behaviours that the parent is going to resist actively.

Fourth basket, or rainbow basket (sometimes also called the flower basket): The rainbow basket provides parents with the opportunity to re-connect with their unconditional love for the child by prompting them to recall special memories and forgotten qualities of the child. This enables the child to be viewed more holistically.

New Authority: The New Authority emphasises parents' self-control and persistence instead of control of the child, mutual responsibility for escalations instead of blaming the child and holding them solely responsible for family break-down, resistance instead of punishment and transparency instead of secrecy. It is a new model of authoritative parenting that promotes supervision, firmness and discipline, and replaces distance, power and hierarchy used in traditional authoritarian parenting. The metaphor of the parent being an anchor for the child and the importance of social support become central components of a secure parent-child bond.

Vigilant care: Vigilant care consists of three stages that can be compared to a traffic-light system. The 'open attention' can be compared to the green light. Parents keep their eyes and ears open, stay vigilant for any warning signals during routine contacts with the child (school runs, meals). In the 'focused attention' (comparable to the amber traffic light), parents become more vigilant and talk to other people who are closely involved with the child (teachers, friends, grandparents etc). In the 'protective action' (comparable to the red light) parents and their supporters take action (announcement, sit-ins, active resistance, increased visual presence, protective actions). Parents regularly shift between these three positions.

The Four Core Parenting Values (Michael Grabbe):

1. Safety of the child and of others.
2. Developing their full potential and abilities in order for them to have a good future.
3. Having good relationships.
4. Showing respect for themselves, their parents and others.

Graduate Parent Participation: Parents who have completed an NVR programme become actively involved in all aspects of the NVR projects (groups, mentoring, presentations, writing, research) to share their experiences with new parents and others. They combine compassion, empathy, containment and support with the hope that others can overcome hopelessness and despair as well, which new parents to the approach can listen to, believe and accept more easily from them than from professionals.

Connecting conversations (adapted from Uri Weinblatt's 'recovering conversations'): After the deconstruction of old patterns, parents can start developing new ways of being for and with their child and learn to *respond* rather than *react*. Once they are ready, they can rehearse with supporters some new ways of being with their child. Active responsive listening to the child, noticing and naming how the child feels, reflecting on their own or others' relevant experiences (without falling into lecturing and preaching), visualising or naming the child's unmet needs, putting themselves into their shoes and seeing things from their side, empathising and asking for forgiveness are all examples of reconnection. This is not an exhaustive or prescriptive list. Graduate parents' testimonies provide inspiration for new parents, who develop their own ways of applying the NVR principles.

After the deconstruction of old patterns, parents start developing new ways of being for and with their child:

- Respond rather than react.
- Active responsive listening to the child.
- Noticing and naming how the child feels.
- Reflecting on their own or others' relevant experiences (without falling into lecturing and preaching).
- Visualising or naming the child's unmet needs.
- Putting themselves into their child's shoes and seeing things from their side.
- Empathising.
- Asking for forgiveness.

Self-announcement: Parents and carers look in a non-blaming and non-judgemental way at the painful feelings and experiences that stopped them from being effective in their parenting. They commit themselves to being present, aware and involved in changing their own role in the unhealthy escalatory patterns, acknowledging their own capacity and motivation for bringing about change.

Self-care/looking after yourself: Parents make time for themselves and for activities that they enjoy, restoring themselves and enhancing their capacity for:

- Meditation and relaxation ('me-time') to calm down.
- Taking time-out and delaying their response to challenging situations in order to reflect, get support and plan their actions.
- Disconnecting the challenging behaviours from the person who they love and care about.
- Opening up to others rather than keeping things hidden (going public).
- Recruiting supporters and sharing tasks of parenting.
- Listening to their own values, feelings and unmet needs (fears and wishes).
- Letting go of shame and guilt.
- Forgiving themselves, their child and others.

- Choosing to heal and re-connect rather than choosing to distance themselves and dis-connect.
- Telling their stories and name their hurts and unmet needs.
- Making reconciliation gestures and identify opportunities for connecting conversations.
- Re-connecting and re-building the relationship with their child.

Use of mindfulness in NVR: Parents and carers learn different ways of mindfulness as a practice of clearing the mind of thoughts and judgements by being attentive to unconscious processes and bodily sensations, thereby helping them reduce thoughtless and reactive tendencies, which usually evolve from patterns of conflict and which maintain them. Mindfulness helps parents to cultivate their parental presence by allowing them to relax and take care of themselves in a constructive way, and to develop a non-judgemental and non-violent stance towards themselves and others.

References

Abuelaish I (2011) *I Shall Not Hate. A Gaza's doctor's journey on the road to peace and human dignity*. London: Bloomsbury Publishing

Alon N & Omer H ((2006) *The Psychology of Demonization. Promoting Acceptance and Reducing Conflict*. London: Laurence Erlbaum Associates Publishers:

Bauer J (2019) *Wie wir wurden, wer wir sind*. Die Entstehung des menschlichen Selbst durch Resonanz. Muenchen: Karl Blessing Verlag

Bauer J (2018) *Selbststeuerung. Die Wiederentdeckung Des Freien Willens*. Muenchen: Random House.

Boal A (1979) *Theatre of the Oppressed*. London: Pluto Press, new edition 2000

Buber M (2008) I *and Thou*, 2nd edition, Edinburgh: T&T Clark.

Burnham J, Alvis-Palma D & Whitehouse L (2008) Learning as a context for differences and differences as a context for learning. *Journal for Family therapy* **30** pp529–542.

Cardenal E (1976) *The Gospel in Solentiname*. New York: Orbis Books, 2nd edition 2007.

Carlson TS & Epston D (2017) Insider witnessing practices: part two. *Journal of Narrative Family Therapy Release* **1** pp19–38.

Day EM (2014) *A rich portrait of the non-violent resistance multi-parent therapeutic programme. Unpublished thesis*. Professional Doctorate in Systemic Practice. University of Bedfordshire, UK. Available at: http://hdl.handle.net/10547/582696 (accessed February 2020).

Day E, Heismann E & Spyrou M (2007) Non-violent Resistance: Guidelines for parents of children or adolescents with violent or destructive behaviours. Dartford: Oxleas NHS Foundation Trust. Available at: http://oxleas.nhs.uk/advice-and-guidance/children-and-young-peoples-services/nvr/

Day EM & Heismann E (2010) *Non-violent Resistance Programme*. Hove: Pavilion Publishing and Media.

Epston D (2016) The Corner. Re-imagining Narrative Therapy: A history for the future. *Journal of Systemic Therapies* **35** (1) pp79–87.

Freire P (1972) *Pedagogy of the Oppressed*. St Ives: Clays Ltd.

Fromm E (1957) *The Art of Loving*. London: George Allan and Unwin Publishers.

Gershy N & Omer H (2019) Chapter 2: Improving fathers' engagement and collaboration between parents. In: *Non-Violent Resistance: Innovations in practice*, edited by Heismann E, Jude J and Day E. pp29–38. Hove: Pavilion Publishing and Media.

Grabbe M (2009) Es gibt keinen Weg zu einer guten Beziehung – eine gute Beziehung ist der Weg. Bündnisrhetorik und praktische Beziehungsgestaltung von Eltern mit ihren Kindern. *Familiendynamik* **34** (3) 266–274.

Grabbe M, Borke J & Tsirigotis C (Hg) (2013) Autorität, Autonomie und Bindung. Die Ankerfunktion bei elterlicher und professioneller Präsenz. Göttingen: Vandenhoeck & Ruprecht.

Heismann E, Wilson J, Law F, McClay S, Weatherley H & McClay R (Eds) (2013) Non-Violent Resistance. NVR – *Rebuilding Family relationships. How NVR has helped to change life in my family. Testimonies from parents, family members and supporters*. Oxleas, NHS Foundation Trust, Dartford. downloadable at: http://oxleas.nhs.uk/advice-and-guidance/children-and-young-peoples-services/nvr/

Heismann E (2013) Eltern mit- und füreinander: Die aktive Mitarbeit von Eltern im Londoner Programm für gewaltlosen Widerstand. In: M Grabbe, J Borke & C Tsirigotis (Hg.), Autorität, Autonomie und Bindung. *Die Ankerfunktion bei elterlicher und professioneller Präsenz* (pp339–353) Göttingen: Vandenhoeck & Ruprecht.

Heismann E, Rospierska D & Watherley H (2014) Application of the non-violent-resistance approach to gangs. In: *Context* **132** p20–21.

Heismann E (2019) Statistics are needed for the professionals to keep running the course, but it is living proof that keeps the parent attending. In: *Non-violent Resistance: Innovations in Practice*, edited by Heismann E, Jude J and Day E pp221–230. Hove: Pavilion Publishing and Media.

Heismann E et al (2019) A group conversation about parent participation. In: *Non-violent Resistance: Innovations in practice*. Edited by Heismann E, Jude J and Day E pp231–245. Hove: Pavilion Publishing and Media.

Heismann E, Pierzchniak J & Prescott J (2019) Reflections on NVR specialist groups for parents whose children are affected by gangs and child sexual exploitation. In: *Non-violent Resistance: Innovations in practice*. Edited by Heismann E, Jude J and Day E. Hove: Pavilion Publishing and Media.

Hines A (2012) Royal Borough of Greenwich, Ending Gangs and Youth Violence (EGYV) Peer Review. Unpublished Position statement of the Senior Community Safety Officer (Youth Crime Prevention).

Jude J & Rivera-Gould V (2019) Fathering and NVR: changing relationships, engagement and perceptions. In: *Non-violent Resistance: Innovations in practice*. Edited by Heismann E, Jude J and Day E. pp39–50, Hove: Pavilion Publishing and Media.

Körner B, Lemme M, Offner S, von der Recke T, Seefeldt C, Thelen H (Hrsg.) (2019) Neue Autorität. Das Handbuch. Konzeptionelle Grundlagen, aktuelle Arbeitsfelder und neue Anwendungsgebiete. Göttingen: Vandenhoeck & Ruprecht.

Lemme M & Koerner B (2018) Neue Autoritaet in Haltung und Handlung. Ein Leitfaden fuer Paedagogik und Beratung. Heidelberg: Carl Auer Verlag

Lemme M & Koerner B (2019) Praesenz und Resonanz in Supervision. In: Neue Autoritaet. Das Handbuch. Konzeptionelle Grundlagen, aktuelle Arbeitsfelder und neue Anwendungsgebiete, Hrsg, Koerner, B, Lemme, M, Offner, S, von der Recke, T, Seefeldt, C und Thelen, H, pp 343 - 366, Goettingen: Vandenhoek und Ruprecht

Martin-Baró I (1994) Writings for a Liberation Psychology. Cambridge, Massachusetts and London: Harvard University Press.

Mesman J, van IJzendoorn MH & Bakermans-Kranenburg MJ (2009) The many faces of the Still-Face Paradigm: A review and meta-analysis. *Developmental Review* **29** (2) 120–162.

Ollefs B, Schlippe A van, Omer H & Kriz J (2009) Jugendliche mit externalem Problemverhalten. Effekte von Elterncoaching. *Familiendynamik* **34** (3) 256–265.

Ollefs B (2017) Die Angst der Eltern vor ihrem Kind. Gewaltloser Widerstand und Elterncoaching. Göttingen: Vandenhoeck & Ruprecht.

Omer H (2004) *Non-violent Resistance: A new approach to violent and self-destructive children.* Cambridge: Cambridge University Press.

Omer H (2010) *The New Authority: Family, school and community.* Cambridge: Cambridge University Press.

Omer H (2017) *Parental Vigilant Care. A guide for clinicians and caretakers.* New York and London: Routledge.

Omer H & von Schlippe A (2004) Autorität durch Beziehung. Die Praxis des gewaltlosen Widerstands in der Erziehung. Göttingen: Vandenhoeck & Ruprecht).

PACE (2019) *The cry of the Brave And Broken-Hearted Parent.* Pace: Parents against child exploitation publication: www.paceuk.info

PartnershipProjects UK Ltd & Oxleas NHS Foundation Trust conference films and interviews DVD from the First International NVR Conference Beyond Behaviour, London, 2011.The DVD can be purchased from Donna Johnson, Highpoint House, Shooters Hill, London SE18 3RG, donna.johnson@oxleas.nhs.uk

Pearce WB (2007) *Making Social Worlds: A communication perspective.* Malden: Blackwell Publishing

Rosa H (2019a) *Resonanz. Eine Soziologie der Weltbeziehung.* Berlin: Suhrkamp Verlag.

Rosa H (2019b) Unverfuegbarheit, Wien – Salzburg: Residenzverlag.

Royal Greenwich (2012) Strategy for Tackling Serious Youth Violence and Gangs (unpublished strategy paper from the Safer Community Lead, Royal London Borough of Greenwich for the Serious Youth Crime Panel.

Sapir E (1949, first paperback edition, 1985) *Selected writings of Edward Sapir in Language, Culture and Personality.* Edited by DG Mandelbaum, Berkley, Los Angeles, London: University of California Press.

Tomm K, St.George S, Wulff D & Strong T (eds) (2014) *Pattern in Interpersonal Interactions. Inviting Relational Understandings for Therapeutic Change.* Routledge, New York and London.

Tutu D & Tutu M (2014) *The Book of Forgiving: The fourfold path for healing ourselves and the world.* London: William Collins.

Waldegrave C, Tamases K, Tuhaka F & Cambell W (2203) *Just Therapy – A journey. A collection of papers from the Just Therapy Team.* New Zealand. Adelaide, South Australia: Dulwich Centre Publications.

Weinblatt U & Omer H (2008) Non-violent Resistance: A treatment for parents of children with acute behaviour problems. *Journal of Marital and Family Therapy* **34** (1) 75–92.

Weinblatt U (2013) Die Regulierung des Schamgefühls bei intensiven Eltern-Kind-Konflikten. Praktiken des gewaltlosen Widerstands, die die Öffentlichkeit einbeziehen. *Familiendynamik* **38** 62–71.

Weinblatt U (2016) Die Naehe ist ganz nah! Scham und Verletzungen in Beziehung ueberwinden, Goettingen: Vandenhoeck & Ruprecht

Weinblatt U (2018) Shame Regulation Therapy for Families. A systemic mirroring approach. Cham, Switzerland: Springer.

Weinbblatt U (2019) Regulating Shame. In: *Non-Violent Resistance: Innovations in practice.* Heismann E, Jude J and Day E (Eds) pp19-28. Hove: Pavilion Publishing and Media.

White M (1989) Selected Papers. Adelaide: Dulwich Centre Publications.

White M & Epston D (1990) *Narrative Means to Therapeutic Ends.* Adelaide: Dulwich Centre.

Whorf B (1956) *Language Thought and Reality, Selected writings of Benjamin Whorf.* Cambride: Massachusetts: Massachusetts Institute of Technology.

Appendix

'Let your joy be in your journey – not in some distant goal.'
Tim Cook (Apple CEO, 29.03.2018)

In a podium talk at a Chicago high school, from which the above quotation comes, Tim Cook finished by saying: 'Our purpose is to serve humanity'. We could not have better summarised how we approach NVR in writing, teaching and in our work with parents and others.

The journey between editing our first handbook, *Non-Violent Resistance: Innovations in practice* (Heismann *et al*, 2019) and co-writing a book on parent participation with three parents has taken us a year. At the end of 2018 we were asked to write a contribution for the new series Leben, Lieben, Arbeiten (*Living, Loving, Working*), which looks at systemic practice in different and diverse contexts and already contains another book about Non-Violent Resistance (Ollefs, 2018). I was interested because I was keen to introduce German readers to our work with parent participation. The three parent authors of this book were equally attracted to the project. We asked the editors to wait until the handbook was published and then started to meet monthly at a café in the borough where two of the three parents lived. Free parking allowed us a chunk of three hours each time we met. While we were writing and discussing, we thought it would be a good idea to ask the English publisher of our previous handbook whether they might also be interested. And they were. That is how we ended up writing two versions: a slimmer one for the German publisher and a bigger one for the English market.

This English version contains an extra chapter (Part 5) that is not included in the German. It also contains three chapters that were originally included in *Non-Violent Resistance: Innovations in practice.*

We thought that it was a good idea to provide chapters 16 and 17 about parent participation as they are supposed to be read in conjunction with each other. Chapter 16 will give the reader a more in-depth idea of the theoretical and historical underpinnings of participation practices in the social world and in systemic narrative practice and theory, looking at the writing and practice of the Brazilian educator Paulo Freire and of the narrative writers and therapists Michael White from Australia and David Epston from New Zealand. Chapter 17, meanwhile, is the transcript of a conversation about parent participation that I had moderated with 17 parents and seven professional facilitators in December 2017. It traces many of the theoretical ideas for a reality-check and contains answers about the lived experience of parent participation from the perspective of graduate parents who have completed our NVR group programmes, some highly seasoned ones, and new parents, who have only recently come across this model, and from professionals who have worked with parents using the parent participation model in their NVR group work. The interview originally lasted three hours and has much more material about the theme of parent participation, but had to be reduced to fit the restrictions of the handbook.

Chapter 10, about NVR groups of parents, whose children were affected by gangs or by child sexual exploitation, has been included because both issues are referred to in Deborah's and Sarah's stories, and also in part 5 of the current book (e.g. in the comparison between the generic and the specialist groups, where home visits and agency presentations are included, and in Deborah's report about the presentation for the international NVR conference in Malmo in 2016).

This chapter contains a very rich description of parent participation during home visits and group sessions, therefore completing and enriching the previous parts of the book.

We believe that even those readers who have already obtained and read the handbook will still benefit from re-reading these three chapters within the more focused perspective of parent participation.

We believe that our journey with parent participation will continue to give us joy and purpose in the future, and we hope that others feel inspired by this book to try the ideas out for themselves, and to develop their own new versions of it in the process.

Chapter 16: 'Statistics are needed for the professionals to keep running the course, but it is living proof that keeps the parents attending'

By Elisabeth Heismann

Introduction

Over the past ten years, the input of graduate parents has become a central force in the evolution of my own approach to NVR practice and training. Graduate parent participation is also steadily becoming more mainstream within many UK-based NVR practices. The participatory aspect of NVR group interventions makes the approach particularly effective, even with people who have been difficult to reach or have experienced resistance to other interventions. The development of participatory work with graduate parents in NVR has close links with other participatory practices and practical influences, which underpin the concepts of the participatory approach in NVR group work. This chapter looks at the contributions made by Paulo Freire, Michael White and David Epston in relation to graduate parent work in NVR.

I start with Paulo Freire, who developed participatory practice in the early 70s in the field of adult education. I then look at Michael White's ground-breaking discourses on participatory narrative practice and the influences of David Epston's performative processes in narrative-based work. I use these stepping stones to reflect on the relevance of the participatory process, when involving graduate parents in NVR work. My aim is to encourage other practitioners to continue developing NVR as participatory practice by expanding the discourse around theoretical influences on NVR parent work.

Participatory education

The idea of participation and collaboration as functions of the education process entered my life in the 1970s when I was transitioning into teaching in Germany. During this time, I also became a member of a social activist group that was supporting a co-operative of Portuguese farm labourers. 'Soldado Luis' had formed following the 'Revolution of the Carnations' in 1974 and, as a result of the 'land reform', land had been allocated to them which had previously belonged to the Patron. By the time of our involvement, the co-operative's members had started to decide upon and run their own affairs. We helped them farm the cork trees, worked with them in the rice fields, and also contributed financially to their cause.

In 1980, a two-year alphabetisation[1] campaign for adults started in the local area. This work was based on the participatory concepts of learning that were developed by the Brazilian educator Paulo Freire. They had been initially tried out in Latin America and were later adopted throughout the developing world. Freire's approach to literacy was revolutionary as it joined the process of '*reading the word*' with '*reading the world*' (Freire, 1987, p182). Freire called it the 'dialogical active participation method' in his book *Pedagogy of the Oppressed* (Freire, 1972) as it requires a dialogical exchange between teachers and students, where both learn, both question, both reflect, and both participate in meaning-making. The teacher uses the real-life situations of the learners as the starting point for a shared investigative journey that takes place between teachers and learners.

The aim of this method is to help people develop critical consciousness through critical thinking styles, thus finding new approaches to overcoming obstacles that have kept them from moving forward. The process of developing literacy begins with the teachers as investigators, immersing themselves in the communities they want to work with. Their task at this stage is for the teachers, supported by co-investigators (members within the learner group), to collect and develop a list of 'generative words and themes' (Freire 1972, p69) (generative words are words that are relevant to the daily lives of the people). These 'generative words and themes' are 'coded' into materials (pictures, texts, films, drama) that will enable the participants to 'decode', understand, critically examine and reflect on their social reality, starting the process of 'conscientisation'. 'Conscientisation' allows, '*reflection and action upon the world in order to transform it*' (Freire, 1972, p24–28)

Through critical reflection in dialogue and co-operation with the teacher and each other, they start acting on this reality and transform it. This enables them to move from being 'objects' to 'subjects', giving them agency in their own lives. This is referred to as 'authentic praxis' as it emerges directly from participants' experiences. Their narratives are communicated, reflected on and acted on. Reflection then expands to a shared process of

1 According to Freire, education starts with literacy, learning the spelling of relevant words that are shared by the community of learners, thereby developing a growing awareness of yourself and your social world. Naming the world is a step towards *conscientisation*.

'reflection in action'. Participation in the struggle for liberation leads to the development of a stance of 'committed involvement' among both teachers and participants (Freire, 1972, p44). The narratives provide a thread between past, present and future, and serve to free up new possibilities.

> *'Looking at the past must only be a means of understanding more clearly what and who they are so that they can more wisely build the future. They emerge from their 'here and now' situation and start to "intervene" in their reality, as they perceive their situation no longer as "limiting" but as "challenging"'* (Freire, 1972, pp57–63).

Seeing the situation as a challenge allows people to externalise the problem and move away from feeling helpless and hopeless. This dialogical encounter is based on 'love', 'humility', 'faith', 'mutual trust' and 'hope' between teachers and learners leading to non-judgemental 'critical thinking' (Freire, 1972, p65). By externalising their important themes, participants are able to perceive their viewpoints as 'perceptions', enabling them to develop new knowledge about self and the ability to experiment with different perceptions and actions, which Freire calls 'testing actions'.

'Testing actions' are used to negotiate the space between the previously perceived and unperceived obstacles and solutions (Freire, 1972, p95). The dialogical encounter is mutually beneficial. Teachers are *'authenticated in their praxis with the praxis of the people (thinking) with the people, not for the people'* (Freire, 1972, pp100–101). It is essential that teachers approach this process with humility, that they are not prescriptive, self-interested or analytical of the learners, which would be another form of 'domination' and 'cultural invasion' (Freire, 1972, pp122–139). The processes of 'witnessing' enables all the participants, including the teachers and the learners, to become 'co-authors' of the learning and living process, leading to the 'enrichment of both' (Freire, 1972, pp144–48).

In our participatory NVR groups, new participants immediately connect with parent facilitators, who share their own lived experiences, similar to those that the new parents are still going through, thereby enabling dialogue and reflection in and on action right from the start. When sharing about having been in similar places themselves in the past, but now feeling at a different stage in their testimonies and dialogues, parent facilitators are thinking *with* new parent participants with empathy, humility and compassion, and not *for* them, while always foregrounding the new parents' current relevant themes and difficulties. In the following section I will look at Michael White's ideas on participation in the therapeutic context.

'Externalising-the-problem', 'storying experience' and 're-authoring lives': Michael White's contribution to participatory praxis in therapy

During the early 1990s, while training to be a family therapist in London, I was introduced to the innovative approach of the 'reflecting team', which was initially conceived by Tom Andersen and expanded by the Australian writer and therapist Michael White. The 'reflecting team' approach and White's concepts of 'externalising' and 're-authoring' felt like a natural progression from my previous experience of participation and collaborative processes in the co-operative and in the classroom. White describes the approach of 'externalising', where clients are encouraged to 'objectify and, at times, to personify the problems that they experience as oppressive. In this process, the problem becomes a separate entity and thus external to the person or relationship that was ascribed as the problem' (White & Epston, 1990, p38). This process allows that previously perceived inherent or fixed qualities become 'less fixed and less restricting' (White & Epston, 1990, ibid).

The 'problem-saturated descriptions' of life or the 'dominant stories' have led to stuckness, blaming and failure. Externalising makes space for 'alternative stories', for co-operation with others and taking action. Thus clients 'retrieve their lives and relationships from the problem and its influence' (White, 1990, p39). Here the focus is on the person's relationship with the problem rather than on the problem itself (White & Epston, 1990, p40). Although the dominant stories shape people's lives, they *'do not sufficiently represent their lived experience ... (because the 'unique outcomes' which are frequently left out in the re-telling) contradict these dominant narratives'* (White & Epston, 1990, p41). These 'unique outcomes' can be plotted together to form alternative stories.

This process leads to the 're-authoring of lives and relationships' (White & Epston, 1990, ibid). This approach is particularly useful, when dealing with experiences and stories of violence and abuse, where attitudes and beliefs, rather than the violence itself, are 'externalised' (White & Epston, 1990, p49). 'Externalising' can also offer people with conflicting perspectives the opportunity to 'establish a mutually acceptable definition of the problem and facilitate conditions under which persons can work together to resolve their problems' (White & Epston 1990, p54). Drawing from his work with families, White proposes that it is helpful but not necessary for those who have a relationship with the problem to be actively engaged in generating and performing new meanings (White & Epston 1990, p59). He says that, *'it is never the size of the step that a person takes that counts but its direction'*, and that 'unique outcomes' sometimes present themselves in the course of the session or afterwards and that it is the therapist's role to be receptive to any 'news of difference' (White & Epston, 1990, ibid) while the client's role is to start taking responsibility for the problem and *'refuse(s) to co-operate with the requirements of the problem,* [thereby] *undermining it...* [allowing them to foster a] *new sense of personal agency ...* [giving them the tools] *to intervene in their world'* (White & Epston, 1990, pp61–65).

White positions this therapeutic process as a 'counter-practice' to the culture of objectification allowing the process of 're-authoring' through alternative stories, new knowledge and subjectivity (White & Epston 1990, p75). In NVR, the concept of connection before correction enables parents to separate the child from the problem. They develop the ability to make meaningful connections with their child, even when things are difficult, and learn to appreciate connection as more important than correction. An important step is helping them to prioritise or externalise their long list of problems in the work with different-sized baskets using their core parenting values.

In the following section, I will describe how David Epston developed the concept of 'Insider Witnessing Practice' as a counterpoint practice to White's approach.

'Insider Witnessing Practice' as a performance-based narrative approach

David Epston worked closely with White for many years. He developed his concept of 'Insider Witnessing Practice' (IWP) after White's death as a counterpoint to the 'Outsider Witness Practices' (OWP). While in OWP strangers convey regard and respect, in IWP an 'intimate other' not only re-stories but 'performs' the narrative, capturing the 'essence', 'qualities of character' and 'history' (Carlson, 2017, Part Two, p21). The narrative process in art and in therapy allows someone to be simultaneously 'author' and 'character' in their own story, sensing themselves in the process of acting and making (Carlson, 2017, Part Two, p24). Through performance, an 'audience' emerges and through 'witnessing' they are 'brought to tears, become angry and called to some response' (Carlson, 2017, Part Two, ibid).

Intimacy develops in the audience, author, and character relationships, where the client witnesses the performance of their own story as 'not me, but not not me' (Carlson, 2017, Part Two, p25). Epston's IWPs comprises of two acts: in the first act the 'portraying therapist' (PT) is interviewed by another narrative therapist or supervisor as if they were the client, extending the story beyond the 'so-far-known' and including a 'hope-biased counter-history' (Carlson, 2017, Part Two, p27). In the second act, the client or 'person portrayed' (PP), becomes a witness to the 'portraying therapists' performance that was developed in the first act, thereby becoming 'both an insider and an outsider to her own story... [allowing her] to feel and experience levels of self-endearment and self-love that are usually reserved only for respected others ... Mutuality of respect is given abundant expression by the therapist's portrayal and in return, the portrayed person reciprocates by doing something similar for themselves' (Carlson, 2017, Part Two, p28–33).

The witnessing in NVR happens through parent facilitators' testimonies being performed live in front of new parents, where often feelings are expressed in great depth or where sometimes the audience breaks out in laughter in recognition of the similarity of the stories told and lived. In graduation ceremonies, to which guests, supporters and public figures like borough police commissioners are invited, some parents do not feel ready to read out their own testimonies but ask someone else to read them on their behalf. These experiences link with what Epston calls being inside a witness, where you see, feel and hear their testimony.

In the following section, I will explore how the ideas of participation are relevant for working with graduate parents in NVR.

Graduate parent participation in NVR group work

In 2006, I came across the ideas and practices of NVR through a training session with Haim Omer, while working in a London Child and Adolescent Mental Health Service (CAMHS). My colleagues and I were immediately drawn to the approach, as the ideas directly applied to the families and situations we were working with. The first pilot group was launched in 2007. The participation of parents who had 'graduated' (having attended at least five weeks of the programme) was a natural progression for us during the third programme. The regular participation of 'graduate parents' subsequently became the most unique and important feature of our parent groups, inspiring professionals and prospective parents as well as re-inspiring the graduate parents themselves. Within the last 10 years, 'graduate parent' participation has become mainstream in a lot of NVR group work in the UK.

The graduate parents demonstrate and embody the aspects of NVR that facilitate sustainable positive change, which are the level of 'parental presence', 'support', and 'protective action' and the four parental values ('safety', 'developing the child's potential and abilities', 'staying connected and enjoying a good relationship with each other' and 'showing respect for themselves and for others' (Grabbe, 2013, p71). Graduate parent testimonies enable new parents to access these concepts more openly and reframe their critical, defensive, helpless and hopeless perceptions towards a willingness to learn new skills. Graduate parents help participants with the challenges of negotiating the dynamics with the professionals, other group members and the NVR process itself. Being witness to graduate parents who have been able to overcome similar limitations as themselves, allows for participants to go through the process of 'conscientisation', becoming 'experimental' (Dewey, 1938, p79) with interventions into their own realities, using 'testing actions', which can be supported and critically reflected upon afterwards.

Receiving the commitment, humility, wisdom, support, solidarity, hope and love of everyone involved, including facilitators, and experiencing everyone as supporters and equals, cultivates a shared 'quest for information and for production of new ideas' (Dewey, 1938, p79), giving rise to further experiences in which new problems present themselves. This experimental method is a 'continual spiral' (Dewey, 1938, ibid). Graduate parents' participation contributes to the joint dialogical investigation that the group undertakes, where the sharing of 'lived', 'told', 'untellable', and 'unheard' stories (Pearce, 2007, p212) leads to the 'continuous formations' and 'readjustments of selves' (Dewey, 2011, p191) in the process of 'self-actualisation' (Maslow, 2012) and the development of the 'art of loving' (Fromm, 1957) and 'human completion' (Freire, 1970, p24).

The physical presence and spiritual guidance of the graduate parents have an 'anchor function' (Omer, 2011) for the participants. Their support does not replace the role of the professional facilitators or other professionals but expands their 'anchoring function' as graduate parent input is more organic, familiar and accessible than the professionals, even though facilitators often refer to their own parenting experiences in relation to NVR to connect more authentically with participants. The presence of graduate parents offers facilitators another layer of witnessing, which enables them to reflect on and act into their own narratives and approach.

The support function of the graduate parents for others and to each other seems to be the most obvious aspect that parents have identified in interviews, questionnaires or in conversations, exemplified in statements like the following:

> *'I have gained more support from like-minded people who understand what it is I am trying to achieve.'*
>
> *'Just everyone is there to support each other.'*
>
> *'Making a stand helps other people make that stand.'*
>
> *'One person can't change things on their own.'*

'Supporters are vital to NVR.'

'They'll help other parents and they'll help themselves.'

'We are supporters, aren't we, to the programme.'

'We are there to support each other.'

The graduate parents feel their involvement with new parent groups helps them stay persistent with their own families. Graduate parents embody what we try to convey in our teaching of the key principles: 'I am not alone. If necessary, I can draw on social support'. Isolated parents have often imprisoned themselves in order to hide feelings of guilt and shame (Weinblatt, 2016) and initially find it difficult to name any support for themselves or their child. In the safe environment of the group, where they experience solidarity, empathy and understanding instead of the prejudice and judgement that they expect from others, they often learn to trust again or sometimes to trust others for the first time. Professionals often too quickly turn to solutions when they are facing these situations, while graduate parents can more easily identify and empathise with this position of loneliness and low mood as shown in the following quotes:

'I know exactly how they are feeling, how low they feel.'

'I have been stood in your shoes.'

'I thought it was just us and everybody else's family was perfect'

'You can see people begin to understand things more if they speak to somebody who has been actually through it. I can't imagine it without it. It's really an important part of NVR to me.'

'NVR is effective having graduate parents actively involved during the parent groups, as they are the voice that tells the reality of how the NVR tools were used to achieve positive changes with their child's challenging behaviour. Parents relate to this as our stories are real, not from a book.'

The question is: what is there to learn from all the presented historical and current participatory approaches in a contemporary context, where knowledge and resources are banked and accumulated in the hands of few? Freire guided us away from this exclusive banking approach in adult education and enabled teachers and learners to communicate and dialogue at eye-level and inclusively. There can be challenges and pitfalls, as our NVR parent facilitators and professional facilitators regularly alert us about:

parent facilitators can be overused or overexposed, and their enthusiasm to give something back can put them at risk, for example when they venture into other parent's homes on their own or when unfamiliar with organisational protocols or safeguarding procedures. In those circumstances expert knowledge can guide them.

However, we see them at all times as the experts on their own stories and lived experiences, but not on those of others. Externalising problem behaviours and unhelpful, harmful patterns of relating to others and witnessing the experience of others and selves, hearing, feeling and seeing them through performance and enactments have always been our preferred ways of collaborating with parents, guided by the ideas and practices of Michael White, David Epston and others like Augusto Boals' work in theatre (Boal, 2000). We believe that people not only participate in speech between each other, but our own and other people's bodies and feelings need to be equally mindfully integrated as speech in all aspects of our work for a fully participatory NVR approach.

Concluding thoughts

As has become evident, these social cultural and conceptual developments have greatly influenced my own thinking and therapeutic and community-based practices and have directly led me to my conviction in the reciprocal benefits of participatory work with graduate parents in NVR. This chapter has looked at the participatory approach of NVR group interventions as one of the most important parts of the NVR group programme. In our experience of NVR work, graduate parents have enabled us to be particularly effective in recruiting and retaining parents who were reluctant to come in the first place or who did not plan to stay, many of whom have become active and passionate advocates of the approach and are actively involved in the programmes.

The development of this participatory practice has a valuable contribution to make to the discourses around participation in community and therapeutic practice. A greater awareness of the historical roots of participatory practice helps us to think about how relevant participatory practice remains today for social and for self-development. The work with graduate parents in NVR could lead the way forward in this respect.

It is my hope that practitioners of the NVR approach continue collaborating with graduate parents and regard parent participation as a core aspect of their practice.

My heartfelt thanks go to all those graduate parents who have explicitly and implicitly contributed to this chapter.

References

Andersen T (1990) *Das Reflektierende Team: Dialoge über die Dialoge*. Dortmund: Modernes Lernen.

Andersen T (1993) *The Reflecting Team: Dialogues and dialogues about dialogues*. Norton and Co.

Boal A (2000) *Theatre of the Oppressed*. London: Pluto Press.

Carlson TS & Epston D (2017). Insider Witnessing Practices: Part Two. *Journal of Narrative Family Therapy Release* **1** pp19–38.

Dewey J (1938, Free Press edition 2015) *Experience & Education*. The Kappa Delta Pi Lecture Series, Free Press New York.

Dewey J (2011) *Democracy and Education*, Milton Keynes.

Epston D (2016) The Corner. Re-imagining Narrative Therapy: A history for the future. *Journal of Systemic Therapies* **35** (1) pp79-87.

Freire P (1972) *Pedagogy of the Oppressed*. St Ives: Clays Ltd.

Freire P (1974, re-published 2013) *Education for Critical Consciousness*. London: Bloomsbury.

Freire P (1987) *A Pedagogy For Liberation. Dialogues on transforming education*. New York.

Fromm E (1957 Thorsons Edition 1995) St Ives: Clays Ltd,

Grabbe M (2013) *Wo fahren wir hin und wo ankern wir? Vom Navigieren in der Eltern-Kind -Beziehung*, chapter 3, pp 61-84. In: M Grabbe, J Borke, C Tsirigotis (HG) Autoritaet, Autonomie und Bindung. Die Ankerfunktion bei elterrlicher und professioneller Praesenz, Goettingen: Vandenhoeck & Ruprecht.

Maslow AH (2012) *Toward a Psychology of Being*. Start Publishing LAC 2012, USA.

Omer H (2011) *The New Authority. Family, school and community*. New York: Cambridge University Press.

Pearce BW (2007) *Making Social Worlds. A communication perspective*. Oxford: Blackwell Publishing Ltd.

Weinblatt U (2016) *Die Naehe ist ganz nah! Scham und Verletzungen in Beziehung ueberwinden*, Goettingen: Vandenhoeck & Ruprecht.

White M (1989) *Selected Papers*. Adelaide: Dulwich Centre Publications.

White M & Epston D (1990) *Narrative Means to Therapeutic Ends*. Adelaide: Dulwich Centre.

Chapter 17: A group conversation about parent participation

22nd December 2017

Key:

New parent *
Parent facilitator #
Established parent facilitator ^
Professional facilitator ~

Group members

Elisabeth Heismann:	Moderator of the conversation and Professional Facilitator
Dorota Rospierska:	Professional Facilitator
Jacqui Swaden:	Established Parent Facilitator
Pete Brown:	Professional Facilitator
Jeanine Heismann:	Professional Facilitator
Lesley Wyvil:	Established Parent Facilitator
Carly Savage:	New Parent
Sukaena Cally:	Parent Facilitator
Angelique Smith:	Established Parent Facilitator
Linda Cakebread:	Established Parent Facilitator
Sarah Blyth:	Established Parent Facilitator
Chinyere Ikpala:	New Parent
Karina Kelly:	Parent Facilitator
Deborah Frimpong:	Established Parent Facilitator
Allison Rensch:	New Parent
Jane Prescott:	Professional Facilitator
Janet Akortsu:	New Parent
Ashley Farrugia:	New Parent

~ Elisabeth: If you were asked to come up with a motto to describe parent participation as a core principle of our way of doing NVR, what would it be?

~ **Pete:** The glue that binds NVR together.

#**Karina:** Perfect balance, that complement each other, parents and professionals.

^**Linda:** It makes it real for parents rather than just hearing from professionals, who may have just learnt from books.

^**Angelique:** We are inspiring to anybody that participates.

^**Deborah:** I think people are learning through our experience. Learning through experience. Because our lifestyle or life experiences really make a big difference. Because each of us has a different life story.

~ **Jeanine:** It also helps to bridge the gap.

***Ashley:** Parent action in NVR.

~ **Pete:** Parent facilitators keep parents coming to the group.

~ Elisabeth: Have you been to parenting groups other than NVR? How would you describe the difference?

^**Sarah:** I've been to one before. It had no parent facilitators, and it didn't really do much for me. It was more like parents sitting there just discussing the problems that are going on indoors. We had no parent facilitators there.

^**Lesley:** If you've got just the professionals there, it come across as if they are telling you what to do. They're the professionals, whereas when the parents are there, they're not just telling you of their successes and saying, *'There you are, you should do it like this. You should do it like that'.* They will also say, when things have not gone well, and how they have coped, and how they have not coped. And I think it makes it more real, because you understand that it is not always going to work. And how to adapt it for each individual family. If it's just professionals, they're just telling you, *'In this situation, you do it like this. In that situation, you do it like that'.* But it doesn't work. The parents tell you when it does, when it doesn't. What they've done, what they've not done and how they wished it had gone better.

~ **Pete:** It makes it real.

^**Lesley:** Yes, and practical. A professional telling you what to do doesn't mean you are going to do what they say. You've got all that resistance, while when you hear, *'I have tried it. I have done it. It works'*, you're perhaps less defensive.

^**Deborah:** With the parent facilitators there you get the empathy and compassion. Everybody's story is different. I came thinking: 'It is me'. But then when I heard other people, I thought: *'Gosh, mine isn't that bad'*. I still thought it was difficult, but I thought: *'Somebody else is going through worse than me'*. So, I could have a different outlook on my situation and have compassion each week, when I came to hear other people's stories.

^**Lesley:** There is also someone there to break the ice to start with. If you're all going to sit there and say what your problems are, I think I would be very reluctant to open my mouth and I'd think, *'I don't want to tell all these people my problems'*. If a graduate parent tells you how difficult it has been and how they have moved on, you think, *'Maybe my issues are not so bad. Maybe, I could open my mouth and join in.'* So, I think it helps to break the ice quicker, because there is already somebody there who's prepared to open their mouth and tell their story.

~ **Pete:** I run both NVR parenting groups and other parenting groups, where graduate parent facilitators aren't present. I think parenting groups without parent facilitators still have their value if the parents can be mobilised to talk about issues. But it doesn't have the same equal atmosphere. But the biggest thing for me is the dropout rate. With standard parenting groups, the dropout rate is extremely high. With NVR groups, it's very low.

~ **Elisabeth: A teacher for adult literacy learning Paulo Freire called the participation approach *'authentic praxis'*, where professionals work with learners in 'dialogue', which he describes as 'reflection on and in action', leading to knowing oneself and others and to choosing wise actions.**

^**Angelique:** From a parent's point of view, whatever you're speaking about is reality. And they feel it. In most of our cases and with our challenging circumstances, we have a lot of emotion about what we are going through. So straight away, that is, what others would see, especially as a new person, who is going through trauma. They just want to know that there are people who they can connect with, who are actually hearing them. You get a feeling of what they are feeling.

~ **Dorota:** Parent facilitators are in a different emotional place and a different place of knowing themselves, and serve as a very positive example of taking responsibility, as opposed to feeling guilty for whatever the situation is. They speak with the other parents who come from a position that their child has to be fixed and ask them, *'What can you do? What kind of parent do you need to become for your child, to be able to make a positive change?'* The change in mindset is happening through the graduate parents' example, because it is implicit in those parents who are saying, 'I've changed my ways, and it helped my child to follow'. For me, it is about knowing oneself. But you can only do it after you have gone through a journey and have arrived in a different place from parents who are new and still in this very painful place and in the middle of a very difficult time.

^**Lesley:** That is, where you can help to move things along so much quicker. Because you can say, *'I was in that position. I came, because I had a difficult child. But this is what I am doing differently, and this is the result.'* So, I think it helps people to see that it is the way you are behaving towards your child and the way you are behaving in general at home which can change.

^**Deborah:** Yes, it's a conscious decision that you have to make. It's not just the child who's the problem. You're part of the equation, and that's the reality. When you get there, you're thinking, *'Why am I having to do this course? She is the problem. She is the one running away.'* And coming to that acceptance, that it is not just about your child, but that what you've been doing has caused an effect on the child. It's mind-blowing. And then being able to have somebody work with you through that. I remember a young lady – it wasn't when she was talking about all the wrong things that she was doing. It was when she was remembering the good things: *'My daughter was a good girl'.* That was when she broke down and started crying. She went to a place that she had completely forgotten. We think, *'I hate my child. I don't want to have anything to do with them'*. And then NVR helps you to reconnect to that place, where they're a baby, where they're helpless. And you just want to look after them. And then you just reconnect back to their childhood. So, I have got to do everything I can again.

Do concepts like 'dialogue', 'self-knowledge', 'wise action' and 'reflection in and on action' make sense to you? If yes, do they fit with a moment in your experience with NVR, when you thought, 'Oh, that's it?'

^**Deborah:** Yes, absolutely. Initially, you're trying to fix your child. And then you find out that you need to fix yourself; that you're broken. You're a broken person. And because you're a broken person, you were making some choices in your life that were having an effect on your child that were negative and producing this negative effect.

^**Lesley:** I didn't feel that I was broken or that I was doing something wrong. I thought, *'I'm not broken. It's not me who is doing everything wrong. I'm doing some things right, and nobody is judging me for the things that I'm not* *doing quite right for that child. It may have been fine for my other children, but it's not quite right for this one.' So, I actually felt much more empowered, thinking, 'I'm not such a bad parent after all'.*

^**Deborah:** I needed to find myself. I needed to find my brokenness to be able to deal with the situation that I had in hand. When I was writing things down in my self-announcement saying, *'My daughter is like this'*, Elisabeth said, *'Try to write it differently'*. And I had to sit back thinking, *'I have a role in this'*. Whereas, when I first came, it was all her. Everything was her fault. And getting to that place where I asked myself, *'Where did you have any involvement?'* And then having to hold your hand and say, *'Don't feel guilty! You're doing it for the right reasons, but you were doing the wrong things'*. Arriving at a place, where you can bear your soul and say, *'I did not even see this. I missed this completely.'* And then you can start reconnecting again.

~ **Elisabeth: You cannot do it on your own, but only in dialogue with others. And real dialogue requires equality, respect, humility, love and compassion.**

^**Angelique:** It's called, 'the teeth of our people's feelings'. Bit by bit, in whatever way is required at the time, we make sure that we're not making that person feel any guilt, shame or blame in order for them to get through that process.

^**Deborah:** They've already been hearing that shame and guilt. We're helping them to release that.

~ **Elisabeth: How do the graduate parents help with the four core parental values?**

~ **Jeanine:** Protecting children from danger, helping them to develop an independent future, helping them to have good relationships and respect for themselves and others.

^**Angelique:** In our group, there were a lot of safety issues and harm to the parents, and we had to get them to understand that it is a lot more serious when they're getting beaten up by their children than when their children are not putting their socks in a washing basket. It had to be voiced that they need to think about respect, safety and about connecting with their family members. They weren't getting it, until I explained about my situation with my son. And then they understood that, talking about my own child's safety was my input as a graduate parent, and that's when the penny dropped for a lot of the parents in our group.

#**Sukena:** One parent had a child who was looking at something very inappropriate: porn. She thought it was quite funny without thinking about the actual implication. We asked her, '*What if the school sees his phone and asks you about it? Would you still find that funny? It's not your son but you who is responsible.*' And she was quiet. It really impacted and resonated that you as a parent are responsible. And a lot of parents have a bit of a light bulb moment. We used it to highlight safety first.

***Carly:** It's about acknowledging it and putting it into practice.

~ **Elisabeth: The values in NVR are used in a generic way to help prioritising positively rather than negatively that everybody can fit them to their own situation.**

^**Deborah:** I think the values help you to affirm why it's important what you're doing. Because by the time you get to NVR, you're usually in a place where you've almost forgotten about your values, where you're near to hitting your child. By having the values brought back to your attention, you realise, '*This is why I am there, why I am trying to find another solution to help my child*'.

#**Carly:** If the values are there, then comes respect; you learn to love them again and your whole family gets involved. It's working for me, because we've got the values and we're respecting each other, having pleasant times indoors. And we've not had that for a long time.

~ **Dorota:** In my group we've got a few parents whose children are not violent and not expressive. Their problems are rather internalised; kids who wouldn't want to go to school or don't want to leave their room and plunge into depression. And still the values need to be resurrected.

~ **Elisabeth: Haim Omer uses the phrase 'anchor function' that parents have for their children, keeping them in a safe haven. He uses it for parents. Does that also fit for what graduate parents do for new parents?**

#**Karina:** When it came to self-announcement, I was holding on to the guilt. It was so difficult. I felt like giving up. I felt like I couldn't cope any more with his behaviour and all the challenges, and I couldn't do it anymore. I was giving up, but I didn't want to. But that's how bad the situation was making me feel. So getting to the self-announcement and being able to say, '*I feel really guilty*'. And to let go of that, because doing NVR means 'connection before correction'. I realised that I wasn't present, that I was withdrawing myself from my child, from the situation, because I didn't like it. And if I wanted to make a correction to his behaviour, I needed to connect first. And then it worked for me. I want to share that with other parents. So, if I can tell this to other people and relate my situation to them, then I become their anchor.

~ Elisabeth: Michael White calls the process where people separate the problem from the person 'externalising'. 'Connection before correction' is how this is done in NVR.

^**Sarah:** When I use 'connection before correction', I feel like I'm getting more of an understanding from my son. He opens up a lot more and I'm not judging him. I'm not blaming him, and it works a lot better for me. There is connection.

***Chinyere:** It's difficult to separate the child from the behaviour.

#**Sukaena:** I've noticed that parents like it when they hear about your situation, when you talk to them about NVR. It really encourages them. I didn't really understand the impact of 'striking, when the iron is cold'. As a parent, I always felt overwhelmed. You've got to be on top of everything, striking when the iron is hot over a pair of socks on the floor, whereas you could look at it, pick them up there and then and prioritise. I can now pass that on to other parents and tell them, *'How can we let that go and do something else?'*

^**Lesley:** With the connection I always go back to when the baby was first born. You don't expect the child to do anything. And neither do you correct them if they cry at the wrong time. You wouldn't dream of chastising a small baby. I mean, they just cry, and you have to accept it. You have to make that connection first. You're giving them unconditional love, no matter what they do as a baby. You just meet their needs. You just love them unconditionally, and you do whatever you have to do, and you don't expect anything back in return. And there are certain times in life when you have to go through that process. You do it when they are a baby. You do it when you're introducing someone else new into the family. And you do it again when they become teenagers or adults.

~ **Pete:** We have quite a number of parents who have had quite difficult early experiences with their children and quite a lot of trauma.

^**Lesley:** They still have to make that connection later on. You always have an opportunity to make those connections, whether it be, when they are first born, six months old or four. You do have to make those connections.

~ Elisabeth: We have all come across hopelessness, despair, stuckness, blaming in new parents. When a new parent hits all your triggers and your trauma again, how do you, as graduate parent facilitators, manage to stay connected and not go back to where you have been and disconnect?

^Deborah: Angelique once asked a parent who was doing her self-announcement key questions while sharing bits and pieces of her own testimony. You could see the light coming on: *'I can do this'*. And she wasn't able to do that without Angelique, who stayed grounded, while talking through her own trauma. The parent really connected because Angelique used her own story for the new parent's story.

^Jacqui: For me it would be going back to the baskets and saying, *'This is important. This is happening to somebody else now. And this is what needs to be looked after at present'.* And then put that first. That's how I follow through the stages. Yourself and things have improved or are improving. And the situation with somebody else at the present time is far worse or in a different place than where you are.

#Karina: Through completing the NVR process myself, I evolved as a person. And then I'm able, when someone else is talking about their trauma, not to think about my own trauma but to think about how I was in that place and now I am in a better place. So it can work, and I've got to pass that onto them. Because my mentality, my mindset and my beliefs, that it can work, remain in me, and because I've evolved as a person, I don't get drawn into their trauma, into how bad they feel and how bad I felt about myself, whenever I listen to somebody else talking. NVR has taught me new techniques.

#Sukaena: You are passing the baton. NVR helped me, and I want to pass that baton over. And when you pass that baton, there is that connection that you have with those parents. NVR is something that's digested and revisited. With the new parent's trauma, it's like a place where I draw support from the professionals and the supervision is paramount for the parents and for me. When I'm going through my own issues and hearing other people's, I have the support from the others who are more established or more experienced or just in a different place. You draw support from that, using the NVR tool of support. That is what they're there for. Showing others that, when we are doing support in NVR, everyone becomes your supporter. It becomes a continuing domino effect.

^Angelique: I mention to parents right at the beginning, *'I have been in this for five years'.* So I'm giving them a concept, an idea, that it doesn't stop now. The thing that I always say is that I eat, sleep and breathe NVR, meaning that I don't shut down. It is for every situation. My son's situation is always ongoing. I do not stop. No matter what age, no matter where he is at, I'm on it all the time. Generally, it is embedded in me.

^**Linda:** Originally, I did the NVR programme for my daughter, my youngest. And at that point, my second youngest had already left home. But he is now back in my life as a 25-year-old with a drug problem, and I'm using NVR all over again with him. It does, as you say, continue.

^**Deborah:** It's a life style.

~ Elisabeth: You hear and see the parent facilitators give their testimony and experience them with your whole body. How is this different from reading a testimony or watching a video?

***Chinyere:** I find it very helpful to listen to them, because they speak with authority. Obviously, they've been involved in it and are often still going through it. And to hear them speak and go into detail, it brings it alive. You are there with that person. Because they're speaking from a place of experience. It's easier for you to imagine what they are saying, listen to what they're saying. They're more credible. Quotes that are read are also very helpful. But, I think, hearing it directly from the horse's mouth brings it to life that bit more.

***Carly:** When the parent facilitators are talking and telling us their stories, they have a lot of compassion. But it also makes me feel relaxed about not being the only one in that position. And I don't feel judged at all, because they have lived it. They're living it out still now. So, I don't mind, talking about my experiences to them, and I don't feel bad about it.

^**Deborah:** It's common ground.

***Chinyere:** If they're going to open up and share that with you, then you feel more inclined to open up with them.

***Carly:** I'm a visual, face-to-face person. I remember receiving CBT once on the phone. I didn't enjoy it because I didn't know who I was talking to. And I couldn't put this voice to a face. So, it's more heartfelt and more personal. I like the way that some stories are put with humour, some with great sadness. You feel everything, what they felt, a touch of it.

***Chinyere:** When you're talking, you're expressing, and when they're talking, they're also expressing. You can hear the emotion in their voices. Often, they speak with passion. And every parent facilitator's story is different. And the way of dealing with it is different. So, you know that this will be also true for you and for everybody else. So, you just know that it's not a one size fits all. But you can draw strength from knowing that each person has found a way of dealing with it individually.

~ Elisabeth: When graduate parents are giving testimonies, the new parents are 'witnessing'.

~ **Jeanine:** My example of that insider witnessing comes from the graduation ceremony, where some people didn't feel ready to read out their own testimonies but had someone read them on their behalf. That process links with being an insider witness, when you see and hear their testimony.

~ Elisabeth: A zoologist called Adrian Thomas talked on the BBC about how his research on the flight behaviours of birds can be used for the development of drones in the military. He said, 'You do not copy the animal. You copy the design, the principal, of what it was intending to achieve'. How do you link that to your own situations?

***Chinyere:** You don't know how you're going to get on with what they say it is supposed to do. You try it out and then see the results for yourself.

^**Deborah:** You get your own experience from trying out the tools and the information that you receive. And that's what develops your story. Because each story changes. Each person who comes to NVR doesn't have the same story. You have similar situations, but your story will still be different. But the tools that enable you to get to or to overcome each challenge are the same. But how you adapt them will be different. I tell parents, *'NVR is like getting a driving license. Once you get your license, you use it as and when. Sometimes I walk, sometimes I take the bus. I don't always use my car, but if I need to get somewhere quicker, I will use my car. And I will use whatever NVR tools are within my reach.'*

~ Elisabeth: So, you are also saying, 'Even in my own set of behaviours, I don't copy the one tool that I learnt, in exactly the same way. We re-design each time'.

^**Deborah:** That's exactly why NVR has evolved to where it is. The work books have changed, have been adapted and have been reconstructed from each experience.

~ Elisabeth: So there is a design behind it rather than just content.

Deborah: A plane is not going like a bird but is designed to be able to fly.

~ Elisabeth: Deborah, you also used the metaphor of the cake, seeing 'Bake Off' on television and wanting to copy it?

^**Deborah:** I was using the same ingredients, but if you added them differently, at a different time with a different temperature, it would come out differently.

~ **Elisabeth: Are there situations where parent participation may be counter-productive?**

#**Karina:** My children don't go to the school where I am facilitating but there are some parents who do facilitate at their children's school, and where there may be a conflict between their children and the school. That is quite difficult. Or seeing another mum in the playground who you are in parent support with and who you don't want to know your story and your business. That can be a little bit of a barrier. Or if you are from the same very connected community and know each other's family and friends, that can be a barrier. Maybe some parents don't want to share their information with you because there is a connection between you.

~ **Elisabeth: You're all so enthusiastic. You want to help, but how much can you do? Who can you do it with? In which situation could you put yourself or others in danger?**

^**Lesley:** I think there are quite a lot of parent facilitators who need more help with boundaries, perhaps even before becoming parent facilitators. They need to be involved in some discussion around where and when you do parent facilitating. I know somebody who has chosen not to volunteer in this area. She travels to another borough from hers because she doesn't want to be in the same area as her child, sharing stories about her child, about what is private or personal. She said, *'It's my daughter's story, and I'm telling everybody my daughter's story, as well as my mine. I don't want to do that in this area, so I'll go somewhere else and do it there'.*

~ **Jeanine:** And as a school, maybe, we should use parent facilitators whose children have already left the school or who are coming back a year after. Or work with parents of much older children who are put in with parents of Year 7 students (aged 11–12 years), so that there's a big enough gap between the children.

^**Lesley:** There needs to be a bit more thought about that, more discussion. Everybody is so enthusiastic.

~ **Pete:** We have to be sensitive. If there's a parent facilitator who has the same child in the same school as a new parent on the course, how do we discuss that? Does that feel OK or not? Supervision is the key.

~ **Elisabeth: What have you learnt about yourselves in the process?**

***Alison:** When I first started NVR, I couldn't see the purpose of it at all. Dorota asked me to turn up, and I did. And I just sat there and thought, *'My son doesn't hit me or anything like that … I'm not going to fit in here. I don't know if it's going to work. I'll give it another week'*. And at the end, I said, *'I still don't think it really relates, but at least I've got the tools to put in my pocket'*. But going back again this year there's someone in the group who is in the same position as me then, and I could just read her straight away.

#**Karina:** Alison used to be bored. Now she's a graduate parent, and a new parent, who doesn't want to be there, really relates to her. Alison makes that parent want to come back.

^**Angelique:** It's taught me that I've got a lot of other strengths that I never knew I had.

^**Linda:** My confidence, self-confidence, has really improved. Just knowing that you can do things. I think when you have difficulties in the family with the children, it knocks your self-confidence. You feel a failure. You can't get anything right. So, to go through all these processes, and then go on and help other parents is boosting your confidence. It really boosted my self-esteem and helped me get a job at the end of it.

^**Deborah:** I think what I learned from NVR is that it's an ongoing lifestyle. I sometimes draw strength from talking to the other graduate parents. It's a lifetime of networking. We're connected through NVR. I've learnt that NVR is a connecting tool, and not just with my child.

^**Sarah:** What I got from it is keeping NVR fresh in my head. Because when you've just done that once in the group it's easy to go back to your old ways. But by being a parent facilitator, it stays with you.

***Carly:** It's like a refresher.

^**Sarah:** And you're adding to the group.

^**Deborah:** And you're learning more.

~ **Elisabeth:** How can the participatory approach be extended in NVR groups and beyond? Can you imagine it with individual NVR?

~ **Jane:** I think so. I remember doing home visits before the specialist group with a graduate parent. I wouldn't have been able to get through the door without the graduate parent there. I think if there's someone who's especially fragile and not able to access the group at that time, it would be a very useful approach to have a professional and a graduate parent working on a one-family-basis, maybe with a view that they might eventually join a group. It had made a massive difference in how the families engaged.

~ **Elisabeth: What would you recommend to people who want to implement participatory practice in NVR?**

^**Deborah:** Give it a go. Try it, there is no harm in trying!

^**Linda:** You never know until you try it.

*__Alison:__ Don't give up! Keep going!

*__Ashley:__ You've got to complete it. If you don't complete it, it's not going to mean anything.

^**Lesley:** Participate in two groups with graduate parents first because you all need to learn to work with each other. Start with parents who are quite sure of their role, even with different people. Work with somebody at least twice! Professionals also need to know that they need to support their parent facilitators. It's two-way.

~ **Dorota:** We're using NVR on ourselves because we need to be able to connect. How can we NVR each other and effectively support each other?

~ **Elisabeth: Is there anything we have missed out?**

^**Deborah:** I'm grateful for the acknowledgment of our role. If it wasn't acknowledged or recognised, we'd not be where we are. We were all in a place of 'rock bottom' with different stories. It helped me to regain my confidence, my boldness, and say to myself: *'I'm taking this on. I am going to resist. I am going to persist'*. A whole new world opened up for me. From just doing a tick box exercise, it just evolved. And now I have permanent connections that are never going to crumble for me.

~ **Jeanine:** How do we get male graduate parents as a resource to reach out to other parents?

^**Lesley:** Most of the time the men are working.

^**Angelique:** In a lot of the groups, the men who do come often say straight away, *'I can come for a few sessions, but not to all. I have got to go to work.'* That's quite common. Do something separate from what we've got already.

*__Carly:__ The process is much faster when you're together.

^**Deborah:** Spouses should get a taster session – a couple of hours or a condensed session for one day. When they say they can't make it, they're working, you can point out that it's just one session, where you are pulling and drawing in all the key NVR things.

~ **Jeanine:** And address with them, *'How is what you are going to learn today helping you to support the person who comes weekly?'*

^**Lesley:** It's really a case of encouraging them to come. How are we going to get them to a place without making them feel awkward? We have to meet them where they are.

^**Deborah:** There's the male pride issue. My husband is over 50; if there's a young facilitator, he'd be thinking, *'She's never going to tell me what to do. I've had eight children. How many has she had?'* That would be in the back of his mind.

~ **Jeanine:** When referrals come through, think about who's in the network and who are the key people, whether it is a dad, an uncle, a grandparent, a neighbour. Who needs to be involved?

^**Lesley:** It's about how we can get to them. How, where and when we do it.

~ **Elisabeth: What was the most important thing about graduate parents' participation that we discussed today?**

^**Lesley:** That brings us back to the beginning. We are the bridge between the parents and the professionals.

^**Deborah:** We keep it real.

^**Angelique:** We all support each other, because we still have things going on in our lives and our journey. We all stay connected, and that connection is getting across to the groups that we end up facilitating. They can feel that.

~ **Jane:** We were thinking about a motto like glue before. I now think of the word 'cement', they actually 'cement' NVR.

^**Deborah:** It was the acknowledgement of what we are and add to the group.

~ **Elisabeth: Are you now more aware of the added value that you bring to NVR?**

*__Ashley:__ I'm glad I came. Because it's just good to be around people who've been through the same thing. I'm so grateful to have the opportunity to do this NVR course.

***Chinyere:** I'm glad I came as well. Because I've learnt some things that I didn't understand before. What people have said has helped me to understand what I have learnt so far and consolidate it more.

***Carly:** I feel slightly more educated in NVR, and it has refreshed everything again.

^**Deborah:** I'm glad I came. Today has made me excited again that NVR isn't phasing out. If anything, it's alive and kicking and well and going into new dimensions with new people, which is brilliant.

^**Sarah:** And it's forever growing.

~ **Elisabeth: Thank you all very much for your contributions!**

Chapter 10: Reflections on NVR specialist groups for parents whose children are affected by gangs and child sexual exploitation

By Elisabeth Heismann, Julie Pierzchniak and Jane Prescott

Introduction

There is hardly anyone who has not come across headlines such as the following five:

- *'The government must get to grips with youth violence and gangs' (Umunna, 2016), 'Gang members "filming rape attacks on schoolgirls as young as 13 in south Birmingham"'* (Oldham, 2017).
- *'Knife crime up 14% because gang warfare is becoming "embedded in our culture"'* (Walker, 2017).
- *'British youth are "the most unpleasant and violent in the world": Damning verdict of writer as globe reacts to riots'* (Moran & Hall, 2011).
- *'Youth crime soars in last five years as gang culture takes grip'* (Clark, 2008).
- *'Parents* need more help to protect their children from gangs' (Firmin, 2012).

Gangs and child sexual exploitation (CSE) are closely connected to drugs and crime in many London boroughs and some other areas of the UK. The south London borough in which we provide a specialist group was the 19th most deprived out of 326 local authorities in the UK in 2010 (Hines 2012). Of the working age residents in the borough, 4.8% were claiming job seekers allowance[2], of which 12% were in the age group below 24 and of which 37% had been claiming for more than six months (Hines, 2012). Considering these demographics, the attractiveness of gangs to young people, particularly organised crime operating as a business, is not surprising. The borough was ranked fourth highest out of 32 London boroughs for assault and third

2 The London average is 4% and the national rate 3.8% (Hines, 2012).

highest for injury offences. The Safer Communities *Strategy for Tackling Serious Youth Violence* report (unpublished) stated that youth crime accounted for 49.2% of crimes where the age of the perpetrator was known.

Of the three authors of this chapter, two practitioners have been involved in generic NVR group programmes (Day & Heismann, 2010) in this borough for more than 10 years. The third author works as a deputy head in a school for boys with social emotional and mental health (SEMH) difficulties in another borough but wanted to learn about the specialist NVR group programme and used the placement as facilitator as part of her facilitator training.

In this chapter, we will describe an NVR group programme with a specialist focus on gangs and CSE that took place over nine months in a London borough. We will describe the uniqueness of this journey through the authors' own experiences as facilitators, the experiences of graduate parents involved in the processes and our learning, findings and reflections. Finally, we will discuss our vision that NVR is a shared practice with a common language that can be used widely to build safe and connected communities.

The need to develop a specialist NVR group programme

Based on our experience of parents who are known to agencies but who do not meet the criteria to access CAMHS, we came to the conclusion that the generic NVR programme in CAMHS did not meet the additional needs of parents whose children are involved in or affected by gangs or by CSE. Some of the graduate parents from the generic NVR programmes who had children with gang involvement and CSE became involved as co-facilitators in our specialist groups.

Our objectives for the specialist groups were to support parents to accept the risks posed by gangs and CSE, to take a non-violent and committed stand against violence and abuse, to de-escalate conflicts and re-build family relationships, to increase vigilant care and parental presence and to break the cycle of silence, isolation, shame and guilt. We therefore designed the specialist groups based on the generic programme, but we altered it in the following ways:

- We made it a longer programme: 14 weeks instead of 12.
- We included individual home visits for four weeks before the group started. The purpose of the four visits was to meet with the referrer and the family to establish their goals, to start building a relationship of trust with them and to introduce them to some of the NVR concepts. These visits were extremely valuable as some parents were unable to attend the

group afterwards but expressed to us and their referrers that they had found the support from the home visits very helpful. *'I so wish I had been able to attend,'* said one such parent, *'this should be available to all parents who are struggling.'* An additional benefit of the home visits for us all was that we managed to see other family members, including the young people concerned, and often recruited their support for the programme. We also distributed some material and information about NVR, thereby planting a seed for possible future attendance.

- We created a steering group with stake holders of gangs and CSE experts (e.g. the gangs link worker for the borough and the chair of the borough's CSE panel), which met four times during the group: they helped us with presentations and presenters. There was a sense of mutual accountability in which information from the group could inform new ways of working and incorporate innovative perspectives into their own agencies.
- We incorporated presentations from local agencies (outlined in *Graduate parent involvement*, below): presenters from various key organisations made themselves available for half an hour at the beginning of a group evening.
- We gave additional support to group members, including phone calls, home visits and attendance at safeguarding conferences.
- We developed our own vision of NVR as a shared practice with a common language that can be used in specialist contexts to build safer and more connected communities.

The findings and learning points in this chapter are particularly drawn from the last group we ran, which combined parents whose children were affected by gangs and by CSE, but we also include our more general learning from the last five years and how we applied it to this particular group and context.

Graduate parent involvement

As in all generic NVR group work, the participation of graduate parents was key in this group. We included four graduate parents in the specialist group, which allowed us to have two in each sub-group. This inclusivity was an essential component of the programme and is also described as a main feature in the Just Therapy service in New Zealand (Waldegrave, et *al*, 2003). Parents could talk from their own experiences of having their sons in gangs or their daughters groomed and sexually exploited.

One graduate parent said, *'As a graduate parent facilitator I really enjoyed sharing my own experiences with the parents and showing them that it is ok to let the barriers down and break the silence'. Another commented, 'Although I was a fairly inexperienced member of the team, I was greatly valued, and my opinion was appreciated... The parents were able to identify with the graduate parent on an emotional level'.*

Graduate parents participated in a training programme about gangs organised by the borough's safer community team, which all facilitators attended before the programme started. They then came along to the home visits where they often encouraged new participants, particularly those who were reluctant or did not think that they or their children had a problem. One graduate parent was surprised by the differences between the participants of the generic groups she had co-facilitated before and the prospective participants in this specialist group:

> *'I was struck by how different the parents seemed to the parents of the CAMHS NVR course. A 'typical parent' on the generic course seems broken, at the end of their tether, unable to cope and afraid to ask for help. The parents we encountered on the home visits tended to be very strong, protective and defensive of their children. They tended to be secretive, distrusting of professionals, not afraid to say what they think.'*

During the home visits, we often met the young people who were originally referred to us and were able to see them and their 'harmful' behaviour in a new light. As one graduate parent said:

> *'The visits gave a human element to the 'gang' members' who had been discussed in terms of offending behaviour. We were fortunate to meet some of the young people, which was interesting. It gave us an insight into how their parents viewed their young people. Some of them were an absolute pleasure to meet which gave us an understanding of how some parents could be unaware of the gravity of the situations their young people were finding themselves in as the children were hiding their 'street' behaviour from the family.'*

This enabled the graduate parents to edit their own testimonies by also highlighting the positive sides of their own children and how they were initially reluctant to face up to the grim reality of their own children's behaviour outside the home and how the NVR group and the presentations enabled them to face up to it.

During the group programme, new participants sometimes formed their closest bonds with one particular graduate parent, often those who had accompanied us to the initial home visits. They would sit next to their 'favourite' graduate parent or try to grab them for a brief conversation before or after the group, or during the breaks.

Although some new participants shared their weekly news with their favourite graduate parent on a one-to-one basis, it was made clear to all participants at the beginning of the program that all facilitators would discuss any additional information about them and their children in the post-sessions. During the professional presentations, for example in relation to missing children, drugs and the experience of young people with the social justice system, graduate parents would illustrate the more abstract material with testimonies of their own experiences, thus enriching it for the benefit of all involved.

One graduate parent observed how their presence benefitted everyone, including the professional presenters:

> *'I think the presenters benefitted and learnt from speaking to our parents, and hopefully our parents have left the course feeling knowledgeable, empowered and more confident in their parenting skills.'*

The participation of graduate parents diffused any fear that the parents had of being judged or criticised. This raised the credibility of the process and strengthened the engagement of the parents and facilitators with each other and with the programme. At the same time, the facilitating parents needed support, training, encouragement, nurturing and validation of their contribution. Some of them were still dealing with challenging and difficult behaviours in their own children. They continued to use the NVR tools to reconnect with their own children and provide them with healthier ways to respond to their behaviour rather than escalating.

Learning points, findings and reflections

The culture of poverty as an adaptation and a reaction of the poor to marginalisation and deprivation

In our NVR practice, we are particularly sensitive to the lenses or the Social GRRAACCEEESS (Gender Race Religion Age Ability Class Culture Ethnicity Education Sexuality Spirituality) (Burnham *et al*, 2008) – with the additions of 'Employment status' and 'Economic situation' that also applied to our cases.

In our specialist group, there were a range of different classes, cultures and religions, among both participants and facilitators. Poverty was a particularly common factor in this group. In our meetings with the parents, we regularly came across and learned about the culture of poverty and deprivation, as described by Martín-Baró (1996):

> *'The poor live in a different world with their own norms and values and their own characteristics. The characteristic features of the family in this subculture, according to Lewis (1969), are that couples are*

> *unwed; life is centred on the mother, there is no childhood in the sense of an extended sheltered period, fathers are often absent; there is a strong inclination towards authoritarianism; and the emphasis on family solidarity remains largely verbal. Individuals typically have strong feelings of being outcast, impotent, dependent and inferior; they do not have enough impulse control; they are very focussed on the present; they are resigned, fatalistic'.*

Some people felt so ashamed of their deprivation that they would only meet us in a cafe or shop. In some homes, we sat on beds because there were no chairs, nor even any room for chairs. This experience humbled us tremendously and made us much more understanding that the daily basics would need to be catered for first before we could hope to achieve anything else, particularly as the *'attitudes and values of a culture of poverty are being continually caused and reinforced by the normal functioning of the social system … and the social and economic structures produce and perpetuate it'* (Martin-Baró, 1996).

Agencies involuntarily inflicting damage and pain on families

Most of the young people connected to the group were known to different agencies, and their parents were often struggling against these organisations rather than feeling contained or supported by them. During the group process, this relationship was sometimes reversed, particularly if presenters from agencies that parents had experienced as unhelpful before made themselves accountable and available for questions and suggestions and appeared to learn from the parents.

Many agencies often only get a partial view of a problem family, based on the specific task they are charged with, while we got a much more complex story. That is why agencies often do not see how psychological damage is inflicted on more than the person they are engaged with. For example, on one occasion the police raided the home of a family of Muslim faith early in the morning. They made the whole family leave immediately without offering them any shelter somewhere else and without allowing the women to put on their hijabs. This experience punished and traumatised the whole family unit and destroyed any remaining trust in the police and other public agencies.

On other occasions, young people were taken out of their homes to keep them safe and reduce the risk that they might traumatise their siblings and disrupt family relationships.

Managing shame and untold stories

How to hear and manage untold, hidden stories of shame, loss, guilt, pain, isolation and silence and fatalism (Waldegrave *et al*, 2003, p91); while building strength, from a position of powerlessness to empowerment not born on domination and oppression but on developing preferred stories and preferred descriptions.

> *'The greater control persons and groups actually have over their present situation, the less convinced will be their fatalism'* (Martin-Baró, 1996, p217).

> *'Change in social conditions and change in personal attitudes go hand in hand'* (Martín-Baró, 1996, p218).

We witnessed that the shame of parents and their guilt led to feelings of alienation from their children and others. Parents often did not know how to reach out to them anymore and they were left feeling helpless and a sense of loss for their child. We also learned that many parents' and young people's stories had never been heard before, not listened to, dismissed, or simply changed into data, with professionals not taking the time to hear what they had to say (Waldegrave *et al*, 2003).

By sharing their stories within the group, the parents not only learned something, but were teaching each other, the presenters and us at the same time about their humanity. It was a very humbling experience to listen to them sharing such intimate, personal stories of their lives when there were no obvious material rewards for them to do so. We discovered that these parents, against all odds, possessed a lot of resilience. Even representatives of the public in powerful positions (e.g. the lead of the Metropolitan Police CSE unit) wanted to hear the parents' feedback and listened to them with respect and empathy. Parents were encouraged to ask questions of the presenters and tell them their stories, helping to break down the barriers between them and the agencies.

The self-announcement session, in which parents talked about what had stopped them being present and vigilant with their children and where they shared their own traumatic experiences, were particularly emotional and liberating. They were followed by a meditation on forgivingness: forgiving themselves and others and asking for forgiveness from others. Afterwards parents were able to access the announcement and look at their children's behaviour without excuses or condemnation, but with more compassion and empathy, which had previously been blocked by feelings of guilt, shame and loss. The meditations usually fitted to the themes of the evenings, but the forgiveness meditation was the most powerful as it often fitted with unforgiven shameful experiences.

In one example, we experienced the empowerment of a black mother of five children who had been in London for seven years as an overstayer, and therefore had no access to public funds. She demonstrated her persistence in keeping her 15-year old son safe (he was involved in selling class A drugs) by going to meet with her son's drug dealer in McDonalds and demanding that he let her son go. This mother gave a moving testimony at the graduation ceremony about this encounter and how her son returned home afterwards, was put on an electronic tag, and developed a more respectful relationship with his parents and siblings.

Cognitive dissonance

> *'Cognitive dissonance is the psychic discomfort of an individual facing two or more contradictory thoughts that in some way imply an incongruence or inconsistency within the self'* (Martín-Baró, 1994, p155).

A cognitive dissonance can be resolved by changing one or the other of the dissonant thoughts through a change in beliefs or behaviour, or new concepts can be added. Family therapists call this concept 'strange loops' (Pearce, 2007). The group process enabled many of these cognitive dissonances to be unpicked and replaced with new stories and understandings. For example, young gang members would often overcome their feelings of compassion by justifying their violent actions with loyalty to their own gang and 'demonising' the others (Alon & Omer, 2006, p1). Another example are the girls who are recruiting other girls into sexual exploitation in order to gain respect from their abusers.

Surprises

One woman brought her new-born granddaughter to many of the sessions as she was her carer. This baby became an important group member and a powerful reminder of how all the parents felt unconditional love for their children when they were babies and young children, responding to them even when they were screaming and required patience. The baby was therapeutic for the group and when the grandmother got upset and tearful, one of the facilitators walked around with the baby.

Gender stereotypes and other stereotypes

We learned that CSE does not only happen to girls when we came across a 14-year old boy who had been sexually exploited by a 21-year-old man.

We also heard about girls being involved in gangs. Sometimes the children and young people were doing well in school or were respectful, creative and pleasant at home (e.g. helping with housework) despite being in a gang or being exploited.

Action research

The testimony given in public and the children's testimonies during the graduation ceremony were an important component of the course, a piece of 'action research', where the learning was put back into the community. Referrers, friends, family members, some of the young people and representatives from the community and the steering group (e.g. the police commissioner of the borough) listened to the parents' testimonies, gave their own feedback and gave the parents dignity, often transforming the way they perceived each other.

'I met other women there... I thought, 'it is not only me – they do have problems as I do. Because of all the skills I learned – I started to understand that the problem is me, without judging. Maybe she needs my help. So, every time I learned something, I used to go home and explain to her this is what I learned – so what do you think about this? To cut a long story short: I learned a lot and now I can deal with situations with my daughter, even outside my house. The relationship with my daughter is very good. She is very open with communication, which I appreciate.'

Another parent wrote: *'It's a place of calm and stillness now, a real home. A place of safety... I have learned far more about my daughter and being a parent as a result of this programme...'*

What constitutes change and transformation?

The NVR framework was meticulously planned but the outcome was organic. Each part of the programme was equally valued.

The value and ethics-based approach of NVR group work is committed to dialogue, accountability, persistence, mutual learning, reciprocity, inclusivity, liberation, freedom, wholeness and justice, participation, humility, love and respect and a non-hierarchical, non-oppressive, trust-building stance (Waldegrave *et al*, 2003; Martin-Baró, 1994).

A partnership approach aims to work alongside and with parents, collaboratively, rather than doing something to them or for them. We adopted the metaphor of 'weaving' the programme together (Waldegrave *et al*, 2003, p75).

The NVR ethics of partnership, persistence, participation, dialogue and respect enabled parents to open up. They did not perceive us as coming with an authoritative agenda (e.g. to take their children away) but with a real interest to hear from them and about their child. They felt 'looked after' and we encouraged them to look after themselves and to concentrate on what they could do for their child, thereby inviting them to get a different perspective on things. We learned that we had to listen to everyone's language and attend to our own use of language very carefully.

Conclusion

We support the view held by Cressida Dick, Commissioner of the London Metropolitan Police, that addressing the problems of gangs, CSE and serious youth violence is primarily a health problem rather than a Home Office or youth justice problem, with prevention being a better strategy than enforcement (Townsend, 2018).

By investing in NVR as a national framework linking social services, schools, the police and the voluntary sector (as we did in the local steering group that supported our project), not only families would be connected with each other but whole communities. The NVR approach can become a shared language. This language is one of connection and good relationship-building, a language of respect for people's rights, safety and integrity, and a language of shared responsibility.

We would like to close with a quote from a mother who attended the specialist group and embraced the approach: *'I came to the first meeting with two black eyes and a heart full of sadness – I come to the last meeting with a heart full of hope for my son's future'.*

References

Alon N & Omer H (2006) *The Psychology of Demonization*. Mahwah, New Jersey: Lawrence Erlbaum Associates.

Burnham J, Alvis Palma D & Whitehouse L (2008) Learning as a context for differences and differences as a context for learning *Journal of Family Therapy* **30** 529–542.

Clark L (2008) Youth crime soars in last five years as gang culture takes grip. *The Mail Online* **10 November**. Available at: www.dailymail.co.uk/news/article-1084549/Youth-crime-soars-years-gang-culture-takes-grip.html (accessed November 2018).

Firmin C (2012) Parents need more help to protect their children from gangs. *The Guardian* **24 July**. Available at: www.theguardian.com/society/2012/jul/24/parents-need-help-protect-children-gangs (accessed November 2018).

Hines A (2012) Royal Borough of Greenwich, Ending Gangs and Youth Violence (EGYV) Peer Review. Unpublished Position Statement of the Senior Community Safety Officer (Youth Crime Prevention).

Hines R (2012) Royal Greenwich Strategy for Tackling Serious Youth Violence and Gangs (10 – 25 years), Unpublished Strategy Report of the Senior Community Safety Officer.

Oldham J (2017) Gang members 'filming rape attacks on schoolgirls as young as 13 in south Birmingham'. *Birmingham Mail* **15** September.

Martín-Baró I (1994) *Writings for a Liberation Psychology*. Cambridge, Massachusetts and London, England: Harvard University Press.

Moran L & Hall A (2011) British youths are 'the most unpleasant and violent in the world': Damning verdict of writer as globe reacts to riots. *MailOnline* **10** August.

Pearce WB (2007) Making Social Worlds. *A communication perspective.* Malden, MA: Blackwell Publishing.

Royal Greenwich Strategy for Tackling Serious Youth Violence and Gangs (unpublished).

Townsend M (2018) Knife crime needs public health strategy, says London police chief. *The Guardian* **6 January**. Available at: https://www.theguardian.com/uk-news/2018/jan/06/knife-crime-metropolitan-police-cressida-dick (accessed November 2018).

Umunna C (2016) The government must get to grips with youth violence and gangs. *The Independent* **22 February**.

Waldegrave C, Tamasese K, Tuhaka F & Campbell W (2003) *Just Therapy – A journey. A collection of papers from the Just Therapy Team, New Zealand.* Adelaide, South Australia: Dulwich Centre Publications.

Walker P (2017) Knife crime up 14% because gang warfare is becoming 'embedded in our culture'. *The Telegraph* **29 April.**